MATT RUDD is senior writer at the *Sunday Times*. In the name of journalism, he has worn a short skirt in public, had a tour of a £300,000 lettuce shredder and stood outside Pippa Middleton's book launch for six hours in the freezing cold. In the name of this book, he has spent the last two years on the road with binoculars, a notebook and many Red Bulls. Follow him without the need for binoculars at @mattrudd

'An opportunity for the English to laugh at themselves. And to show everyone else how mad and brilliant we are'

Jeremy Clarkson

'Matt Rudd makes the voyage around England with the eye of a more frivolous, lighter weight George Orwell . . . It's quirky, irreverent, ironic, allusive, boyish, self-mocking, shrewd and funny. Foreigners, bless them, don't write like this'

Country Life

'Highly entertaining . . . In his hands, and contrary to received wisdom, sarcasm is one of the higher forms of wit . . . Rudd's book is a warm and witty celebration of England and the English, filled with a succession of eccentric characters . . . proof that comedy is one of the things the English are very good at indeed'

Sunday Times

'Perfect for dipping in and out of on, say, your commute to work, as each chapter is pretty self-contained. But be prepared to laugh out loud. And start nodding and thinking, "Yep, I SO know that person," every few seconds . . . Clever and witty, but oh-so-true, you'll love this fab look at our nation'

Sun

Also by Matt Rudd

William Walker's First Year of Marriage: A Horror Story
William's Progress

THE ENGLISH

A Field Guide

Matt Rudd

WILLIAM
COLLINS

William Collins
An imprint of HarperCollins*Publishers*
77–85 Fulham Palace Road
Hammersmith, London W6 8JB
WilliamCollinsBooks.com

This William Collins paperback edition published 2014

1

First published in Great Britain by William Collins in 2013

Illustrations by Simon Spilsbury

A catalogue record for this book is available from the British Library

ISBN 978-0-00-749047-9

Set in Minion by Birdy Book Design

Printed and bound in Great Britain by Clays Ltd, St Ives plc

MIX
Paper from
responsible sources
FSC™ C007454

Find out more about HarperCollins and the environment at
www.harpercollins.co.uk

For A & A,
former proud owners of a Datsun Cherry

CONTENTS

Introduction 1

1. The Sofa 13

2. The Kitchen 41

3. The Garden 67

4. The Commuter Train 95

5. The Office 119

6. The Pub, the Club and the Balti House 143

7. The Shops 169

8. The Sports Field 195

9. The Motorway 225

10. The Beach 249

11. The Bedroom 273

Afterword 303

Acknowledgements 309

INTRODUCTION

THE BEST THING about going on holiday is coming home.

Sorry.

Too much.

The fourth best thing about going on holiday after the blue Mediterranean skies, the blue Mediterranean pool and, umm, the blue Mediterranean cocktails is coming home. It can't just be me who finds comfort in the sheeting rain welcoming you at the airport, the heavy spray sheering off the lorry failing to overtake the other lorry on the way up the M23, the abundant grey-greenness of home.

I once lived a long way from England but a very short way from a totally tropical beach, the sort of beach they use to flog Bounties. That wasn't all. I had a girlfriend who was at least 80 per cent as lovely as the Bounty ad girl. I was twenty-something, living the coconut-confectionery-based dream. Work. Beach. Sleep. Work. Beach. Sleep. Work. Beach. Throw a shrimp on a barbie. But then something awful happened. I started to miss the grey-greenness. You

1

get tired of the blinding yellows, the gaudy blues, the sun-baked ochres of the tropics. You yearn for sludgy colours. Sludgy colours are calm and dependable. A sludgy colour won't kiss your wife all the way up her arm and then offer her a private tour of its island on the back of its Vespa.

So I gave up that tropical beach and my 80-per-cent Bounty girl with her apartment just back from the shore-line and her nice teeth. I swapped parrots for sparrows, vegemite for Marmite and thongs* for mittens-on-string. I came back to the drizzle. So far, so straightforward. This is something any English person will understand, unless you claim to be an English person who likes unremittingly good weather and Christmas lunch in the cruel sunshine of the southern hemisphere in which case you are either lying, not really English or my Geordie friend Donna. But there's more to it than a lemming-like enthusiasm for bad weather. There must be.

Over the last eighteen months, I have been on a journey into the lives of the English to find out what makes us tick.

As far as possible, I have adopted the David Attenborough approach to this journey, as opposed to the Bruce Parry one. Attenborough looks at his gorillas through the under-growth and whispers peeping-Tomishly to camera. Parry is more hands-on. If a tribesman inverts his penis, Bruce inverts his too. At no point during the making of this book have I inverted my penis although I did go to Blackpool

* I never wore a thong, just to be clear. We're just painting a picture here.

2

which turned out to be almost as painful. Of course I am an Englishman so it's a bit like a gorilla whispering peeping-Tomishly about gorillas. But I have tried to be an objective gorilla.

'Don't be too sarcastic,' the editor had said controllingly at the outset. And, if I'm honest, I thought that would be a tall order because, as we have just this very minute established, I am English, not counting the strong influence of the Armenian grandmother.* Ask anyone English about their fellow Englishers, and you'll be hard-pushed to find an enthusiastic, glowingly complimentary response. We're just not like that. We're not like our altogether more up-beat, high-fiving, group-hugging, group-whooping cousins across the Atlantic. In very exceptional circumstances, as demonstrated every sixty years or so, we can set out the bunting and flags, and sing anthems with tears in our eyes. And we are quite capable of thinking we're better than lots of other countries or that if we aren't, it's not our fault, it's the government's or Brussels'. But you will never find us climbing lampposts and chanting England, England, England like they climb street lights and chant USA, USA, USA. Not unless we're coming back from a football match, but that's different.

---

* Her influence explains the nose, the wire-brush hair and one of the seven reasons I had to turn down an offer of marriage while on assignment in Azerbaijan. The man offering me his daughter would have been rather upset when he found out I was part Armenian. And he had a very big, curved knife.

Despite all this, I did set out with a vague hope that it might not be all bad. That the drizzle pervading the soul of English life might not be quite as unremitting or even as real as you'd think. It might just be part of our weird, self-deprecatory national psyche. Miserableness could be the national glue. It is certainly the starting point of every comedian, sitcom-writer, columnist and hairdresser in the country (or maybe I just have an unusually grumpy hairdresser). It's what you talk about when you bump into someone you know only vaguely on the train – how miserable everything is. But it might just be a magic kind of miserable, strong enough to bind us together but superficial. Underneath the miserableness, things might not be that bad.

This journey is not a geographical one. Well, it is – I have travelled the length and breadth of this green and grey land – but it is not structured that way. There will be no chapter on northerners or the Cornish or the Norfolkers or, worse, the bequiffed, beplimsolled Shoreditchers. Our regional peculiarities will emerge patchily and unpredictably, just as they do in life. Any attempt to compartmentalise a nation in that way is doomed to ridicule. If you're Cornish, you know the way you speak is funny. You don't need me pointing that out. And I don't need you coming round my house with your all right my handsums and your pitchforks.

This is also my excuse for focusing on the English as opposed to the British. Like it or not, Alex Salmond, much of what we will discover applies just as well to the Scottish or the Welsh as it does to the English. This is not a travel guide, it is a journey into our daily lives, and I would suggest, dangerously, that the biggest variations between our homes, our working lives and the way we roll at the weekend still come from 'class' as opposed to which corner of England, or, for that matter, Britain, we inhabit. And even that generalisation is fraught with exceptions, the most significant being that we live in homogenised times. We watch the same television, buy the same BOGOF cheese from the same supermarkets, read the same S&M books. Still, there are some national differences. And frankly, the boiling rage certain elements of these fair isles will work themselves into if they are, once again, lumped into a big book of Britain suggests they feel strongly about it. So we will save Scotland and Wales and, yes, Northern Ireland but not Gibraltar, for another day. Where I use the term British rather than English, it is not because I am forgetting this solemn pledge. It is simply because whatever we are discussing applies to the lot of us. Don't get your sporran in a twist.

This is a journey not around the geography of the land but the geography of our lives. We will be snooping, whisperingly, around our homes, our offices and wherever we go at the weekends. We will be looking at how we cook, eat, drive, work, sleep and, ahem, other stuff some of you might still do in bed.

We begin on the sofa which is, by the way, an almost impossible place about which to be unsarcastic. My problem, not yours, but really, it's not easy. This is the place English people spend the vast majority of time when they aren't sleeping or working. Four hours a day on average. Four hours. A DAY. Not counting students. Not counting Jeremy Kyle. In the living room, we find sloth. But, is it really that bad? This is the question I will be asking, as unsarcastically as possible, as we focus our creepy binoculars on every aspect of English life. Is the metaphorical self-flagellation (it is just metaphorical, isn't it? Please tell me it is) every time we slump into the well-worn curve of our beloved zero-per-cent-financed three-seater really necessary? To find out, my fellow Hobbits, we must step into the world of sofas and sitting rooms. We will stare at people through their living room windows and decide if it really is as dire as everyone says it is.

From the sofa, we will travel to the kitchen where, if anything, the default view is more miserable still. What's the first thing that comes into your head when we mention the English and food? Rosemary jus, you say? Are you kidding? You are kidding. Funny. For me, it's the microwave meal. The sound of lids being pierced. The four-minute ping. And other things: plastic cheese, 'energy' drinks, none-a-day, sugar, sugar, sugar, and the only thing worse, sweeteners. Distraught parents pushing turkey twizzlers through school fences because Jamie tried to make their children eat vegetables.

If the sofa is sloth, the kitchen is gluttony. Gluttony and envy. My kitchen surface is more expensive than your kitchen surface. My coffee machine is more industrial than yours. My Ocado delivery is bigger than yours. The venison I'm serving at my dinner party went to a better school than your venison.

Again, is it really that bad? We shall, fellow questers, find out. With any luck, those twinned sins of envy and gluttony might just be dismissed with a bish bash bosh and a ping.

By the time we step into the garden, it gets easier to be upbeat. We're very good at gardens. Not miserable at all. A little neglectful perhaps. Those weeds aren't going to strangle themselves. But we like to potter in our small corner of England. It has not ever been thus. Unless you were Downton posh, gardens used to be the spare cupboard, a place to chuck stuff or grow potatoes or hang knickers or all three. Now we have Monty Don and herbaceous borders and, forgive me for this, rooms outside. We have pretentions to aristocratic horticultural grandeur. This has grave implications. There are issues out there in the green and pleasant garden that are more frightening than anything we find inside the home.

And then we must leave the home altogether because, you know, mortgage. How do we get to work? In the very old days, we walked. In the old days, we took the penny farthing. Now, we commute. I think we all know that no one is going to have a good word to say about commuting to work at half-five in the morning. But we will try in Chapter Four.

And I think we all know that we are drifting further from the French model of the working week (thirty-five hours, two hours for lunch *avec du vin*, a whole summer off) to the terrifying American model of the working week (bagel at becubicled desk, no holiday ever, death by Power-Point). But we will grin and bear it as we investigate office life in Chapter Five.

And I think we all also know that when we go out drinking after work, we are very naughty binge drinkers and if we're not careful we will burst our livers. But we will line our stomachs and pack the Alka Seltzer for a tour of pub and clubland in Chapter Six.

From there, we reach the weekend. Ahh, lovely weekend. We will begin in the shops because if English people spend their evenings on the sofa, they spend their weekend in the shops. Shopping centres are the new cathedrals. Internet shops are the new internet cathedrals. The high street is dead. Thanks a lot, supermarkets. Grumble, grumble, grumble.

The other thing some of us do is play sport. Or watch other people playing sport. Before we pretty much won the Olympics, you could have expected a chapter being rather downbeat about this nation's sporting prowess. Well, not any more, Sonny Jim. Okay, a bit Mr Jim because we will tackle football as well as running, skipping and jumping. And if you're expecting me to maintain the rosy hue of optimism all the way through a football match, you've got the wrong writer.

The other, other thing we love to do at the weekend when we're not shopping or watching other people kick balls is drive around a lot. We love our cars, don't we? Really love them. Polish-them-at-the-weekend love them. Spend-more-time-admiring-their-contours-than-our-wives' love them. We will explore traffic jams, not just from the back of them but also from the control room designed to prevent them. And we will spend an entire day – twenty-four hours, a practical short-break – at Newport Pagnell services, the first motorway service station to open to the public and a five-star award winner, no less, in the category of toilets. That seems perverse, you might think. If you're going to construct an argument about how things aren't as bad as they seem, you wouldn't go to Newport Pagnell. But no. You're wrong. Silly, wrong you. Motorway services are the starting point of all childhood holiday memories. The sense of movement, new frontiers, adventure, the outside chance of being given a tin of sweets covered in flour, all start at Junction so-and-so of M-whatever.

And then, after all that hard slog through domestic bliss, work horror and the social whirl of your glamorous week-end, we'll find ourselves at the beach. Great Britain is the ninth largest island in the world. In other words, we are not Robinson Crusoe. You could easily go a year without catching a glimpse of the coast. But at the end of every road, apart from the orbital ones, is a stretch of brown sand or pointy pebbles. The English beach gets a whole chapter of its own because it is a particularly good spot for English-watching.

It is the wildebeest equivalent of open savannah. There is nowhere to hide. We will see how different one wildebeest can be from another wildebeest, how some will pay £22 for fish and chips, and we shall reach sweeping conclusions just in time for the final chapter . . . the bedroom. About which we need to say little for now other than that I have left that chapter to last because I always put off the most awkward, embarrassing, teeth-clenchingly, eyes-to-ceiling tricky jobs until the very, very end. Because I'm English.

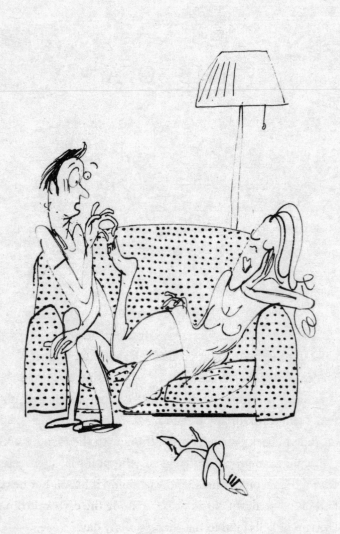

THE SOFA

SHE SLEEPS WITH A PILLOW over her head. Not on the sofa. On the bed. It's not a deal breaker. You learn to live with stuff like this in a long-term relationship and I'm quite sure she has a long list of things I do that annoy her, not that I can think of any offhand. Maybe my devil-may-care attitude to sock pairing. Or the thing with the toenails and the bath. Something foot-related. The point is, she sleeps with a pillow on her head and, last night, it fell off her head and onto the alarm clock, thus subduing the early morning chirrup of bells vital to the success of my day.

'Why was the bloody alarm clock on the floor?'

'Why was the bloody pillow on your head?'

I drove to the station car park, grabbed my bag out of the boot, slammed the boot shut and realised my phone, my wallet and the only car key we possess since someone (me) lost the spare were all still in the boot. The boot was locked. The whole car was locked. I have no idea how it happened. It is not an especially paranoid car. No middle-of-the-night alarm calls. No ejector seat. Half the time, the central locking doesn't work at all but this morning, of all mornings, it had worked a little too well.

I borrowed a phone and called home. She, the cat's mother, the wife who sleeps with a pillow over her head, did not answer. She never does the first time ('because it's probably one of those recordings of someone trying to sell me something'). It's not a deal breaker. You have to learn to live with . . .

I borrowed a twenty off Mehmet, the Coffee Guy on platform one (more of him later), and caught the very late train.

And missed the bus.

I ran through the streets in the brutal early morning sunshine, cursing all who stood in my way. I jumped over a flowerbed, a shih-tzu and three old-age pensioners, but I still missed the meeting I really absolutely couldn't miss.

'I told you we should have got another key cut,' she said when she finally answered the phone.

There was no time for a proper lunch which is a shame because there had been no time for breakfast and, what with all the running and jumping, I was beginning to see tiny blue and purple patterns in my eyes. I ate a Scotch egg at my desk even though the Scotch egg was old and the average desk is less hygienic than the average toilet, according to a survey I wish I had never read.

In the afternoon, everyone shouted at me, I had no time for a cup of tea, and then I left. I missed the bus. I ran through the streets in the brutal late evening sunshine, jumped over the flowerbed, the pensioners and, exotically, a miniature schnauzer, and arrived at the station. Then I realised I had left my train ticket on my desk. My wallet was still in the car. Flowerbed, pensioners, schnauzer, schnauzer, pensioners, flowerbed, train.

'The AA man managed to break in. I've left the key under a crisp packet by the fence post in the hedge nearest but one from the car,' the cat's mother had said earlier. 'You really should have got another key cu—'

No sign of the key, even after a twenty-minute finger-tip search, the kind they do in Danish police dramas the second time around after the first crime-scene team hadn't done it thoroughly enough and the murderer, who is obviously the best friend of the dad, is still free as a bird, looking ambiguously at things off camera. I put on a white paper boilersuit, a mask, the works. No key.

I borrowed a phone.

'No, a Mini-Cheddars packet.'

'You said crisp packet.'

'Yes.'

'Mini-Cheddars are not crisps.'

'Don't be ridiculous.'

'They're a savoury biscuit.'

'Could I possibly have my phone back?'

Home at last, tired, sweaty, tetchy. But it's all okay because there she is, waiting for me, right there in the sitting room like she always does. Still as beautiful as the day we first met. Well, okay, not quite. She's lost her shape a bit. She sags in the middle. The wear and tear is becoming quite embarrassing, socially. It's only a matter of time before she has to be replaced with a new, fresh, firmer model. But at least she's comfortable and familiar.

My sofa.

The only thing I can count on at the end of an exhausting day. Feet up, rubbish telly on, glass of half-price supermarket wine (full price established at full price in 321 stores from March 7 to March 7 and a bit) within easy reach, bottle a little further away because I'm not a complete alcoholic. Ahhhhhh.

And then she walks in. My wife, not the sofa.

'Darling, I didn't hear you come in,' she says. 'How was your day? Nightmare about the keys.'

No. Don't do it. Please. She's walking towards me, not quite apologetic even though everything that happened today was her fault, but certainly conciliatory. Which means she wants something, something I really don't want to give her, not after the horror of my day, not when it's only a Tuesday and it's not her birthday.

More smiles. Closer now. Right past the uncomfortable other sofa, the leather one that neither of us likes, bought in our twenties when we lived near Islington and thought style was more important than content.

'Budge up.'

No. Please.

'Move your legs over.'

No. That Medusa smile. The snake hair. No. No.

'Do you mind if I just put my feet up?'

Aaaaarrggghhh.

'Could you just rub there for a minute? Right on the ball. I've had such an exhausting day.'

HOW DO YOU SIT ON YOURS? Do you have your bottom near the front and your head at the back so your chins rest on your manboobs and Pringles have no easy route down your gastrointestinal tract? Do you perch nervously like you're in the waiting room of a cut-price vasectomy clinic ('30-day money-back guarantee if you're not completely satisfied with the results')? Perhaps you sit in the osteopath-endorsed manner, bum back, spine straight, eyes in line with a point two-thirds of the way up the television screen, a bowl of raw vegetables and low-calorie dips next to the subscription-only ashtanga yoga magazine you're about to read from cover to cover. No, of course you don't.

Do you have a footstool? Tell me you don't. Thank God. Do you use the arm of the sofa as a footstool? And as a result of your misuse of the arm of the sofa, do you fall asleep in the third or, more recently, second quarter of the hour-long programme you knew you'd never get to the end of? At 10.35 p.m.? Or, if we're going to have a really honest relationship throughout this book, 9.35 p.m.?

Me too. Apparently it's to do with biorhythms. It's not even our fault.

You can learn everything you need to learn about the English from the comfort of a sofa. If you are a glass-half-empty anthropologist, what you learn will be bleak and soul-destroying. It will confirm what you always suspected: that we are, as a nation, finished, ruined, kaput, over. In the Victorian era, people sat upright in wing chairs and settees while inventing things, writing things, reading things and plotting the further expansion of the empire. Now, we slouch and just look at the state we're in. Look at it. We haven't colonised anything in ages.

During the Olympics, more people watched more television than ever before. How ironic. Until someone invents a way to get fitter just by watching people do exercise on television, and no, *Tree Fu Tom* doesn't count, things will only deteriorate.

Glass half-full time. This is not our fault. If you try to sit straight on a modern sofa and you are not an Ewok, your head hangs over the back. This is uncomfortable, unbecoming and possibly dangerous. For the sake of your vertebrae and your reputation, you adopt a more oblique angle. You accept the laws of gravity and lie down. If sofas had proper backs, everything would be different. England could still be great.

We must also accept that the 'three-seat sofa' is a lie. Put three people on a three-seat sofa and the chap in the middle is a lemon, a social pariah, an unassimilated odd-ball. This sort of thing might be acceptable in places where there is no concept of personal space such as Italy or Bluewater, but in most parts of England no one sits in the middle seat of a sofa. It's almost as antisocial as taking the middle seat on a train which is almost as bad as hyper-hidrosis. No, the 'three-seat sofa' is a one-seat sloucher, a Trojan bed, the chair equivalent of a computer-generated Stoor Hobbit whispering, 'Have a little lie down, my precious. You deserve it.'

The Age of Slouchery is not our fault.

I AM STANDING at the entrance of DFS Carcroft in South Yorkshire. You might not think that sounds exciting but you'd be wrong. DFS Carcroft isn't just any DFS. It is the original DFS. It was on this very piece of ground in 1969 that Graham Kirkham, a twenty-four-year-old son of an Edlington miner, started Northern Upholstery, forerunner of Direct Furnishing Supplies, in a room above a snooker hall. If Kirkham had passed his O-levels and joined the Royal Air Force as he'd always dreamed, I would not be standing here shaking hands with Darryl, DFS Carcroft's manager. And this might not be the Age of Slouchery. But

Kirkham fluffed his O-levels and here we are, Darryl and me, definitely shaking hands.

As we walk in, we are assaulted by a suite of sofas so red, you could murder an entire South Yorks family on it and no one would notice. I point at it derogatorily and ask if anyone has ever bought it.

'Reds are very, very popular,' says Darryl, apparently unperturbed by the redness.

'Really?'

'Well,' he replies obstinately, 'people buy what they see. I could put it out in orange and they'd buy it. I could put it out in green with pink spots, and they'd buy it. We could do one in tennis-ball yellow, and they would buy it. We once did pink and purple suede. And guess what?'

'They bought it?'

'They bought it.'

'I don't believe you.'

Buy now. Pay in 2087. This gorgeous three-seat recliner, yours for just £499 (£87,000 after event). DFS. Making every day more comfortable. Exactly what is the event after which a DFS sofa will cease to be £499? It has to be something pretty significant. A mere nuclear holocaust wouldn't be sufficient. There would have to be asteroids at the very least or a sudden folding of the time-space continuum unforeseen by everyone including Stephen Hawkins but not the marketing team at DFS.

It is not important. What is important is that Catherine and John are about to buy a sofa from Darryl. They haven't bought a new sofa for twenty-five years. This makes them unusual. According to Darryl, a huge chunk of his customers come back every couple of years to 'update their front room'. That's what people do these days, he says with a philosophical cough.

'We're modernising,' says John, with a sideways glance at 'the wife'.

'You're not going for that one, are you?' I ask.

We're standing next to a three-piece monstrosity in white leather. It has a high back, I'll give it that, but it's so high, it's reminiscent of a very old people's home. That is not all. There is also a chair that matches and something else, something quite different, something Darryl tells me, with an embarrassed smile, is called a cuddler. It is a circular, rotating, padded seat with a semi-circular back, half-*Total Wipeout*, half-Elizabeth Taylor's Cleopatra eating grapes. Tarty, with delusions of not being tarty.

'And you're going for the cuddler?' I ask John.

'Goodness, no,' says John, fiddling with the control on the sofa. John has his limits.

The Navona, as the sofa suite is called because who knows why, maybe the designer had just been to Rome, is one of DFS Carcroft's top sellers and it comes with an optional 'power recliner'. We have a discussion about the pros and cons of a button that makes the sofa recline. Catherine argues that if you're spending £200 on this facility, you're saving £49 because the puffie, by which I hope she means footstool, is £249. 'You don't need a puffie if you've got a power recliner,' she clarifies.

'But you can't get an electric recliner,' I say. 'That's the beginning of the end.'

John nods. Catherine digs in.

'Well, it's not for me, it's for me mam,' says Catherine. 'She's disabled. And so are you, John.'

We both look at John.

'That's true,' he says, tapping his leg which makes an un-expectedly tinny sound.

This is just typical, telling a one-legged man he can't buy an electric recliner.

'Sorry, you're disguising that well,' I say. 'I suppose you can get the button.'

John had an accident down mine. His damaged leg got an infection. It wasn't treated properly. He lost his leg. This was years ago. He's allowed to have the button – but unless you're over ninety or you have a valid blue badge for your car, you are not. While Catherine and John fill out their paperwork, I tackle Darryl. Not literally, he doesn't deserve that. But he does have to answer for his part in Slouchgate. Baron Kirkham is a billionaire, a collector of old master paintings, including Constable's *View on the Stour*, which cost him £6.7 million, and Gainsborough's *Peasants Going to Market*, a snip at £3.5 million. That's a lot of sofas. And Darryl is his henchman. Explain yourself, Darryl.

'People aren't couch potatoes,' he says, self-reclining on another bright red monstrosity. 'We're working harder than ever, aren't we? People round here used to do shifts. You'd work from six till two or seven till three in the mines or the steelworks but then you'd be off. I work from eight until six. A lot of people work longer hours than that. And they commute. They have twenty minutes for lunch, they rush around and when they get home, they're knackered. The last thing they want to do is sit in a formal dining room having a formal dinner. I don't know about you but I just want to slump and watch some telly.'

COUCH POTATO is a pejorative term. In 2005 exasperated representatives of the potato industry even stood outside parliament and the offices of the *Oxford English Dictionary* campaigning to get it changed to couch slouch.* They obviously had a chip on their shoulder.** But if Darryl is right and we're only reclining because we're working harder than we ever have, then we should regard the term more warmly. We should embrace it. Think of the couch potato as over-worked and undervalued, the exhausted jacket-and-tie potato of the twenty-first century.

* 'We are trying to get rid of the image that potatoes are bad for you,' said British Potato Council head of marketing Kathryn Race. 'Of course it is not the *Oxford English Dictionary*'s fault but we want to use another term than "couch potato" because potatoes are inherently healthy.'

** Sorry.

And how bad is sitting slumped in front of the television anyway? Technically, quite bad. Dr John Ott, a scientist and photographer who spent a lot of time not watching television and a lot more time studying the health effects of sunlight and artificial light, lived to the ripe old age of ninety. One can only assume he followed the lessons of his own research. In 1964 Dr Ott read an article in *Time* magazine reporting how two doctors were studying a group of children, all suffering from fatigue, nervousness, headache and insomnia. They could find no root cause until, eventually, they realised the children were TV addicts. They were watching between three and six hours of television a day during the week and up to ten hours a day on the weekend. A complete ban on television was applied and within three weeks the children were as right as rain.

Dr Ott decided to take these findings a step further. He got hold of a very large colour television and covered one half of its screen with solid lead to block radiation. The other half was covered with photo paper to block light. He then planted six perfectly innocent beans in pots and placed them in front of the lead side, and six more in front of the photo paper. After three weeks, the beans in front of the lead were absolutely fine. The beans protected only by the photo paper showed an excessive vine-type growth. 'Furthermore, the leaves were all approximately three times the size of those of the outdoor plants and those protected with the lead shielding,' wrote Dr Ott.

Now, if the gardeners among you are thinking this is excellent news and that you will immediately desist from reading this chapter in order to relocate your pot plants to the sofa, stop it. This is not the lesson we are to draw from Dr Ott's runner-bean couch potato experiment. We are meant to conclude that too much telly is bad.

To ensure no one mistook his experiment for an excellent way to grow veg, Dr Ott replaced the beans with some rats. Two of them got the photo paper side, two got the lead. The rats without the lead protection became hyperactive and then lethargic. After ten days, Dr Ott had to push them to make them move about the cage which, for the non-scientific among you, is not good. To ensure this wasn't just a bad batch of rats, Dr Ott repeated the study. The next group of telly-addicted rodents died within twelve days. Two others became so lethargic that Dr Ott rushed them to Evanston Hospital. I'm sorry to say the rats didn't pull through. Autopsies revealed brain tissue damage.

But let's not panic. These kids, these rats and these runner beans were American and it was ages ago. Older cathode ray televisions might have emitted radiation but since Dr Ott's experiments the amounts have reduced drastically. Plasmas and LCDs aren't nearly so bad. And if you don't believe me, you can always log on to www.emfblues.com and buy yourself a Crystal Catalyst˙ Dielectric Resonator ('tested by independent third party laboratories for over twenty years') to suck up all the gamma rays.

Still, we now watch an average of four hours two minutes' television every day, according to the Broadcasters' Audience Research Board. That's more than twenty-eight hours every week, a mere afternoon short of our world-champion cousins across the pond (who manage thirty-three hours). Despite all the other modern distractions such as iThings and laptops and Kindling, it is the most we have ever watched the box. This, and Angry Birds, and Netflix, is why English sofas have dips in the middle.

Almost 60 per cent of UK households have two or more televisions. More than 10 per cent have four. Only 3.5 per cent have no televisions at all and most of them live in isolated farm buildings in Norfolk.* The most watched genres are entertainment and drama. Two-thirds of telly watched is now commercial. In the last year, there were 984 billion individual views of adverts, the highest ever recorded. The industry calls these views 'impacts'. We watch forty-seven ads a day. That's a lot of impact.

This coincides with a rather depressing study by the University of Queensland which concluded that every hour you watch television, you shorten your life by twenty-two minutes. And no matter how much you love Noel Edmonds,

---

* I have friends in Norfolk and they have a television although I recently discovered that my great-great-great-great-great grandfather was a reaper in Reepham, and he didn't have one. Also, the people of Norfolk have other things to do in the evening (see Chapter Eleven: The Bedroom).

Deal or No Deal is never going to be worth that sort of sacrifice. Dr Lennert Veerman, who ran the study, argued that this 'ubiquitous sedentary behaviour' is a 'public health problem'.

I phoned Dr Veerman and pleaded Darryl-from-DFS's case. We are tired. We stand on public transport. We sit in traffic jams. We work hard. We rush around. We eat lunch at our unhygienic desks while managing spreadsheets and Gocomparing car insurance and fending off the people who bullied us at school but now want to be friends with us on Facebook. Please don't make us sit around actually talking to each other in the evening. Please let us watch television.

Dr Veerman doesn't give an inch. He does not buy Darryl's argument. He doesn't buy mine either when I suggest there must be some benefit to all the rushing around that counters our sedentary evenings.

'The effect of television on mortality is independent of the physical activity a person performs,' he says belligerently. 'Running around all day would partly offset the increasing risk associated with television viewing, but it would not cancel it. What you gain in health during the day, you can undo in the evening. And I am not sure there is much evidence that the English are really more physically active now than they were in the past.'

Perhaps Dr Veerman is unaware that I have only recently taken up jogging. Or that you have only recently taken up walking around in full-body Lycra with those tiny little pink dumbbells. (Well done you, by the way. You're doing great. The pounds are falling off.) So let us spend an evening with an average, typical English family, plucked at random, using my English Plucking Randometer, and find out if our slouchery is really so bad.

SATURDAY EVENING in a village in Kent, and Simon and Sian are 'enjoying' a 'quiet' night in with their four children, Louis, fourteen, Sam, twelve, Gabi, ten and Theo, six. Gabi has baked cupcakes for my arrival, Theo is attempting cartwheels but the two oldest boys are distinctly less excited by the prospect of having to talk to an actual person. Sam is on his iPad 2. Louis is on his iPhone 4. I suspect they're only in the room because of some puce-faced, three-line whip issued moments before I arrived. Their parents, friends of friends of friends, look a little nervous. It has taken months to convince them to let me witness their Saturday night. They would rather the rest of us didn't know.

'So if I wasn't here, you'd all be sitting together, holding hands, a happy family in a front room watching a programme involving dogs, fat opera singers and Simon Cowell?' I ask with a mouthful of cupcake.

'We're not idiots!' shouts Theo. Theo is trouble.

'Theo!' chorus his parents. Then Mum suggests that while Dad still tries to encourage communal viewing on a Saturday ('It's family bonding,' he interjects with a wry smile), she gave up a long time ago.

'Things have become easier since we moved the piano to Lock 'N' Store,' says Dad. 'The music room has now been renamed the front room and the kids can go in there and watch their stuff.'

'And you watch the *X Factor*,' says Mum helpfully.

'Dad loves the *X Factor*,' say the children loudly, for the benefit of the tape.

'I don't watch telly,' says Louis, a bit muffled, trapped as he is between an enormous pair of headphones.

Here is an anomaly. An English teenager who has shunned his generation's obsession with the small screen and found other things like books and harpsichords and the musings of Plato to fill his time.

'No, I watch most stuff on the internet – iPlayer, YouTube, films.' Last week, he downloaded *Schindler's List* but played Xbox during 'the boring bits'. His parents look appalled.

Louis estimates he spends at least five hours a day looking at screens. He has 654 friends on Facebook but gave up the social-networking site for Lent.

'It was getting a bit much,' he admits candidly. 'I was coming home from school, going straight to my computer and staying on it until I went to bed. The first week without it was quite hard but then it got a lot easier.' Facebook Anonymous.

'Are you also on Bebo?' I ask, nodding like I'm like hardly bovvered – and he snorts.

'You just got a teenage snort,' says Mum, who is so far proving just as subversive as the teenager.

'What did I say?'

'Beebo shut ages ago,' says Louis, snorting again. 'It's Facebook, BBM, Tumblr, Skype.'

Sam, the twelve-year-old who has remained quiet/fused to his iPad until now, joins the snorting so I ask him whether he watches *X Factor* with his dad. Before he can answer, his mum outs him as the family's most obsessive Skyper. 'Sometimes he'll go up to his room to do his homework and a few minutes later you'll hear maniacal laughter,' she says. 'I'll find him video-chatting with his friends.'

'Yes, but I also do my homework,' says Sam.

'He cheats!' says Gabi treacherously.

'It wasn't like that,' says Sam from the family dock. 'I was just looking around the internet for information for an essay and found the exact same question on the Cambridge website. There was this button that said, "Solution", so I clicked it. The answer was right there so I cut and pasted it into a Word document and sent it in.' Your Honour.

'What mark did you get?'

'I haven't had it back yet.'

Gabi and Theo are on Club Penguin. 'It's Facebook for under-tens,' says Dad. 'It's a sort of chat room.'

'Yeah, full of forty-two-year-old men,' mutters Louis.

'I've got a puffle,' screams Gabi and then attempts to explain what a puffle is, what it has to do with penguins, how it all works and I feel at least a thousand years old.

'Shouldn't you be out climbing trees?' I ask.

'It's good for them,' says Dad, that wry smile flaring again.

'Dad's very naughty,' shouts Theo, already fully versed in sarcasm at such a tender age, and then walks, expertly, across the room on his tiptoes, making the rest of the family burst out laughing. Even Louis breaks away from his iPhone to smirk. I suspect they are exaggerating their gadget obsessions for my benefit. When I leave, they'll have a good giggle about how much their digital existence scandalised me.

All the same, this household has a total of six laptops, five games consoles, five mobile phones and three televisions. They use fifty-five gigabytes of data a month. The last time they went on holiday, the children asked if the hotel had wi-fi before they asked if it had a sea view. The family had eight devices plugged into the hotel's wireless network. They can't remember much about the sea view.

So we need to take stock.

'Imagine if you were growing up in your dad's era,' I say. 'Only three channels on the telly and the middle one would have been grainy. No computers, no iPads, no Skype, Facebook, Puffles or Bebo . . .'

Snigger. (riso em silêncio)

'Okay, well, none of that. Nothing. How do you think you would feel then?'

Sam puts down his iPad and fixes me with a suspicious look.

'Would I be travelling back to the 1970s or would I just be there?'

I'm onto him. I know where he's going with this. 'You'd just be there,' I counter. 'So you can't say, "I'd love it because I've always wanted to have a go in a time machine."'

'Okay then,' he says, unperturbed. 'I wouldn't be bothered because I wouldn't know any better. I wouldn't miss my iPad because I wouldn't know about it.'

Genius. They all are. Smart. Funny. Quick. They might not be brilliant at climbing trees but when was the last time you absolutely had to climb a tree? It's not like we're Canadian. There are no grizzly bears in Kent.

'My FEAR IS that these technologies are infantilising the brain into the state of small children who are attracted by buzzing noises and bright lights, who have a small attention span and who live for the moment,' Susan Greenfield, the Oxford University neuroscientist, was quoted as saying in the *Daily Mail*.

Simon and Sian's four super-cyberkids aren't that bad. Short attention span? Maybe. Infantilised? Nope. Is it really that bad, I ask Baroness Greenfield, reading back the quote to her.

'Well, the way they've put it makes it sound like you'll turn into Peter Pan the minute you switch the television on,' she says. 'My view on technology is that it is neutral. It's meaningless to claim a computer or a television or a car is good or bad. The issue is more how often it's used and how it's used.

'The funny thing is, every moment you're alive, you're rewiring your brain. People assume we have fixed brains and fixed personalities so the idea that a computer or a television is rewiring them seems outrageous. We are constantly rewiring. Your brain and my brain have rewired since we started this conversation.'

'I can feel it,' I say encouragingly. But I can't. I've had three coffees and I'm still a bit slow. Mornings. Hard-wired. Middle-aged.

'Given this astonishing plasticity of our brains, it's a given that if the environment impacts so strongly and if the environment is changing, then our brains will change. So the real question is how does it change? Is it good or bad? How do we harness the good? How do we minimise the bad? In a sense I've been misquoted.'

So is television detrimental or not?

'To say something is detrimental implies you are making a judgement and you have a set of values. So I'm nervous about saying it's detrimental. If you are spending five hours a day in front of a screen, it means you are spending five hours a day not doing something else. Now, if you were going to spend those five hours bashing up old ladies then of course it's better for you to be in front of a screen, but let's assume that wasn't the plan and instead you wanted to climb trees or talk to people face to face. Which is better?'

I suggest that I have excellent hand–eye coordination and a very low entertainment threshold as a result of the many hours I spent in the mid-eighties mastering Horace Goes Skiing, Frogger and the seminal Chuckie Egg* on my ZX Spectrum 48K.

'Yes, but why should two dimensions stimulating only hearing and vision outcompete three dimensions and five senses? Clearly the screen is giving you a different experience that is compelling. What does a Playstation [or Spectrum] give you that tree-climbing doesn't? We need to work that out.'

OUR LIVING ROOMS ARE SHRINKING. It started happening in 1975 and it hasn't stopped since. In the small hours, when we're all asleep and nobody is looking, the walls move in, millimetre by millimetre. That's what that scraping noise is. The shrinkage is directly and inversely proportional to the increase in television screen size. You can now buy a fifty-five-inch television for less than £200 in the supermarket. So we are all sitting closer to televisions that are bigger. Why haven't we noticed the walls are moving in?

* The fact that Chuckie Egg only made thirteenth place on *Your Spectrum's Official Top 100 Games of All Time* remains a travesty. Number One was 3D Deathchase in which you were a motorbiker chasing two other motorbikers. It wasn't very 3D.

You might not have noticed because you are a Kazakh-stani oligarch or a Premiership footballer's wife and you have a separate media room. I haven't got a separate media room. I'd like a separate media room but there are many things that need to happen before I get one including the death/departure of my wife and/or the freezing over of hell. She does not grasp that media rooms are 'important' and 'no longer the preserve of the super-rich', even though the property section of the *Sunday Times* quite clearly states that they are.

'What is normal or necessary has changed,' Ed Mead, of Douglas & Gordon estate agents, tells the newspaper. 'As television sets are now so large, buyers are more likely to be thinking of where to put the telly when they view a home. It can be a good idea to swap a storage room for a media room. It improves saleability.'

Maybe the rest of us haven't noticed the moving walls because of IKEA, the magical land of Toftbos, Apskars, Smygs, Fartfuls and the 50p hopefully-horse-free hot dog from heaven. IKEA took the English Royle Families and Hyacinth Bucket and chucked them out with the chintz. For that we should be truly grateful. But not for other things.

Before IKEA, you could buy a piece of furniture that had already been made. I'm sure you are absolutely fine with flatpackery but I have, in the past, been overwhelmed. I have been that little Morph scratching its head at the start of an IKEA instruction manual. I have the Allen-key scars to prove it. And I have smashed the front windscreen of a

Vauxhall Corsa while trying, desperately, to prove to a told-you-so girlfriend that I was right: the Billy bookcase would fit in the boot. But that was a decade ago, when we were IKEA novices. Now, I relish it. I have an Allen-key drill bit. If you shut your eyes and listen to me building something from IKEA, you would think you had been transported to the Ferrari garage at Silverstone. Bzzzzfffft. Bzzzffft. Bzzzzzfffft. Bzzzzfffttttt. Clear!

Un-flatpacking, I have mastered. And when I spend an entire day getting hunger-anger in IKEA and then an entire other day building all the stuff I built, it means I'm not watching television or beating up grannies, which keeps Baroness Greenfield happy.

There is one nagging doubt though. Have we really chucked out the chintz? Do we now live like Swedish architects, sipping espressos on low-backed sofas with maybe one, tiny sheepskin rug in front of the incredibly minimalist wood burner while our wives pop out in the Volvo for some lingonberry jam and meatballs? Or are our lives just as cluttered, only more Swedishly?

TWO-THIRTY IN THE AFTERNOON. IKEA Thurrock. Essex. Former county of chintz. I am in the car park accosting people wheeling out great trolleys of stuff like they've just been told a hurricane is coming and after tomorrow there will be no more affordable yet cleverly designed furniture.

'Hello, I see you've bought quite a lot of stuff there. Can I ask what you came in to buy?'

'No.'

'Please?'

'A bookshelf.'

'And what did you end up buying?'

'A hotplate, twelve wine glasses, a picture frame, a toy train set, a children's tea party, a pop-up tent, a cutlery holder, some cutlery, a television stand, a towel rail, a magazine holder, umm, what's that, yes, a sort of step thing, 600 tea lights, a pot plant I don't like, a mirror I don't need, a family-size pack of frozen prawns and this cow-skin puff.'

'What about the bookshelf?'

'They were out of stock.'

This man, whimpering a little, was not alone. In one hour, I spoke to eighteen trolley-pushers. Only two-thirds had got what they came for but all of them had bought more things on impulse. At least half were already regretting it.

'I always buy a bag of tea lights,' says one woman, shaking her head. 'I don't even know why. I'm not a student any more. I've been married for fourteen, no fifteen years. I haven't had a candlelit dinner since the 1990s. Why do I keep buying tea lights?'

'I came for a sofa,' said a man, almost in tears. 'I'm leaving with a bath mat.'

'And a hot dog?'

'Yes, a hot dog.'

'But not the meatballs?'

'No, not the meatballs.' IKEA

We still have clutter, just cleaner-lined clutter. Which leaves us precisely where? Slumped on our auto-reclining DFS sofa, brain-damaged like unfortunate rats in a 1960s experiment, hemmed in by IKEA chintz, massive televisions and hand-held gadgets only children, children who should be climbing trees, understand. But don't despair. It's not that bad. DFS Darryl was right. The sofa is a place to escape from the stress of the day. We collapse on these surrogate beds because we're working harder than ever to pay mortgages that are larger than ever to banks that are eviler than ever.*
We commute longer. We sleep less. Work and rest. No play. No amount of Mars Bars will help us now. Unlike the sofa.

In ye olden dayes, we would have gathered around a candle to squint at the latest instalment from that cliff-hanger Hardy, and maybe you ladies would have done some needlework and maybe us men would have smoked a pipe and wished we had something more comfortable to slump on after a long day at the candlestick-maker than this straight-backed sofa made of wood and spikes and cold sores.

It's not so different now.

We're just squinting at iThings instead of papyrus and our cliffhangers come courtesy of emotionally constipated Danish detectives rather than emotionally constipated Dor-

---

* England is the only country in Europe where we work longer hours than we did in the 1980s. Well done us.

set shepherds. It's bad but it's not the end of the world. And besides, there's another reason we haven't noticed our shrinking sitting rooms. It has nothing to do with Toftbos or Fartfuls. It's because the room next to the sitting room is growing. Why? Bish, bash, bosh.

THE KITCHEN

All I ever wanted to do was to make food accessible to everyone; to show that you can make mistakes – I do all the time – but it doesn't matter.

JAMIE OLIVER, who obviously hasn't tried
my filet au poivre au chocolat de mignon

'HELLO.'

'Helloooooo.'

'Oh, I love your hair.'

'I love your dress.'

'This old thing?'

'Hahahahah.'

'Hello.'

'Here's some plonk.'

'Oh, you shouldn't have. Come in, old chap. How's work? Still doing the commute? I only go in four days now.'

We were here in the far reaches of Surrey partly to catch up, partly to have dinner but mainly, as it transpired, to bask in the magnificent glow of their interior-designing brilliance. We began by being made to admire their new staircase and the living room, which looked to me exactly the same as it always had done but now 'talked far better to the rest of the ground floor, don't you think?'

Then came the pièce de résistance. The new kitchen-dining room. Sorry, not 'room'. 'Space'. It was hewn from granite, glass and irritating brand names. In the gleaming black surfaces, I could see my reflection and the depths of despair with everything that is wrong with the world. Our host, wearing an apron that said, 'I'm not drunk, I'm still drinking,' made his way to the cooker on the pretence of needing to stir something while the guests said 'ooohh' and 'ahhhh' at some spatulas and a sink tap.

'Check this out,' he said, pointing at an enormous black circle on the wall behind the hob.

'Blimey. What is it?' we chorused dutifully.

'It's a cooker hood.'

'But it's on the wall. Shouldn't it be above the cooker?'

'Ha! No.' He grinned with Machiavellian delight. We had fallen into his trap. 'It features Perimeter Aspiration. It sucks air across the entire surface of the hood, thus increasing the effective extraction area when compared to a traditional fan. Canapé anyone? Shall we move through to the reception space?'

After we had been given time to absorb the full provenance of the smoked salmon on the blinis, we settled down in the dining space for dinner. There was cold soup, obviously. And then beef Wellington and I won't bore you with where the beef came from because I suffered enough for all of us. Suffice to say the cow had been on first-name terms with Hugh Fearnley-Whittingstall.

My fervent prayer for the cooker hood to malfunction during 'plating up' and suck the entire dinner into its surprisingly quiet vortex had gone unanswered. It's not that I despised our host. It was simple jealousy. Pathetic.

Fortunately, the Wellington was burnt. Not irredeemably so but the beef was grey not pink. Our consummate host and already tipsy hostess exchanged heated whispers by the wonderful kitchen tap (this is the problem with a 'space' as opposed to a 'room' – much harder to conduct the vicious dinner-party argument in secret), before he stormed back to the cooker to check on the roasted root vegetables. Overcooked too. The final straw.

'It's all ruined,' he whispered shoutily at the crisped carrots.

'How's your house?' said the hostess to us, deflecting.

'It's all bloody ruined,' he repeated and started banging his head on the six-zone convection hob.

'It's fine,' I replied to the hostess as she took a large swig of gratuitously expensive wine (not half-price in any stores for any amount of time ever). 'We might have to get a better cooker hood now though. Hahahahaha.'

'Hahahahahaha.'

The main course was tense. Various people made half-hearted attempts at compliments, small talk and neutral yet entertaining political discourse but the tension killed them off and after a while there was nothing but the actually-not-that-quiet hum of the cooker hood to fill the void. All those present hoped that the pudding would be something simple and stress-free.

It was a chocolate soufflé.

As it rose, so did the mood. The host, still fragile, got back his swagger. The doors at the other end of the dining room fold right out to bring the garden into the house. The architect did a skyscraper in Shanghai and the entrance to a Tube station. Amazing that we could get him. The under-floor heating has actually cut the heating bill.

Then he opened the oven to retrieve the soufflé. A freak spiral of cool air trapped between the cooker hood and his annoying apron must have hit the front of the now-doomed dessert.

'Noooooo!' he cried in slow motion, lifting it out onto the polished black surface sourced from a particular quarry in southern Sicily. And then the rest of it went down too, just like the *Titanic* but with chocolate instead of a string quartet.

'The lighting in here is wonderful,' I said, looking at the ceiling. 'Is it eco?'

'I told you not to do the bloody soufflé,' she said, pouring another glass of wine like she was trying to put out a forest fire. 'I don't know why you couldn't have bought the Heston lemon tart like I said. No one would have known.'

He looked at her.

She looked at him.

'They would have known,' he said eventually, and stormed out. The cooker hood was turned off. We ate the puddle of soufflé in silence. It was delicious (the chocolate was from Costa Rica).

THE TWO GOVERNING PRINCIPLES of the English kitchen – showing off and cutting corners – have enjoyed a close relationship since the first English caveman hid the packaging for a Waitrose hairy mammoth risotto and tried, unsuccessfully, to pass it off as his own.

It was only after the Second World War that things really began to get out of hand. In 1949, with the arrival of the all-new pressure pan, it was all about showing off because you could save time. 'The housewife of tomorrow will be pressure-cooking minded,' boasted an ad for Prestige cookers. 'For pressure-cooking is speed cooking. The most delicious meals take only a matter of minutes to cook, fuel bills are cut drastically. Delightfully simple to use and a pleasure to own.' Yay for the housewife of tomorrow. You go, girl. No mention of house husbands, of course. It just assumes it will be the women having all the fun.

Fun and danger. Because there was always going to be a cost if you're trying to save time and show off all at once. Life is just like that. With pressure cookers, even the new-fangled compact ones of 1949, it was the chance you might die horribly in a lamb-flavoured explosion. It was the rattling and the hissing that was the clue. Manufacturers tried to explain away the rattle and hiss as 'essential to the design'. What an enormous relief.

Only recently, six people died and seventeen others were injured when a pressure cooker blew up in a Phnom Penh market. Okay, it was an industrial pressure cooker and one suspects regulations in a Cambodian marketplace might not be quite as stringent as those here but it's the same principle. Pressure cookers. Pressure. Cookers. 'The explosion was so powerful that it lifted me off my bed when I was asleep,' said seventy-eight-year-old Hok Meng, who lived across the road from what had been a noodle shop. Hok was lucky. The whole chimney exploded, firing a metre-wide chunk of Cambodian masonry through the zinc roof of an adjacent launderette where two of the victims were sleeping.

Similarly, my mum had one in the seventies. Nobody died but we were never allowed in the kitchen unless we were wearing full body armour. Once, we had to clean meatloaf off the ceiling. After that, the bomb disposal robot always went in first. He was fearless.

In the grand scheme of things, death and/or horrific steam burns were worth the risk. A lamb stew in fifteen minutes? A Brown Betty in half an hour? With an exciting, hissing gadget you could tell the neighbours about? Prestige pressure pans sold like hot cakes.

Then Teasmades sold like hot cakes. The Teasmade was a life-changing invention, worthy of entry into the Hall of Life-Changing Stuff Invented by the English, next to the bagless vacuum cleaner, the adjustable spanner, penicillin, the Cornish pasty and the guillotine.* In one fell swoop, it (the Teasmade, not the guillotine), answered a question no Englishman had until then dared to ask: could the ancient art of tea-making be easier and more show-offish through the power of technology? Can you refine the agonising process of waking up, getting up, going downstairs in the cold, making a cup of tea and then going back up to bed to drink it? With the Teasmade, the answer was yes. From henceforth, there would only be the waking up and the drinking.

It wasn't done in an Archimedean flash. There was no Eureka moment. No apple fell on anyone's head. A Birmingham gunsmith by the name of Frank Clarke first registered a patent for a Teasmade-type device in 1902. He hadn't cracked the name – he called it 'An Apparatus Whereby a Cup of Tea or Coffee is Automatically Made', which isn't quite as snappy. Over the next sixty years, there were various incarnations. The concept only really became viable in the sixties when someone who wasn't a Birmingham gunsmith decided that electricity might be a more comforting

---

* Yes, Monsieur Guillotine. The Halifax Gibbet was a West Yorkshire forerunner of your 'invention', first used in 1286. It came with a sporting chance. If you could withdraw your head from the block after the blade was released, you would go free. The opposite of bat the rat with an outside chance of a *Last of the Mohicans*-style scalping.

bedside power source than gas and someone from the marketing department shortened the name. Suddenly, no one ever needed to get out of bed again. Civilisation could have ground to a halt.

It didn't. The baby boomers realised there was more to life than tea in bed. They still got up. And then they went further than that. They went too far. They shunned the Teasmade. Why? Why, why, why? It makes no sense. Why did you deprive future generations? It's so selfish. Except maybe you didn't like the dripping noise it made the hour before it woke you up. Made you want to pee. And, of course, it was a bedroom-based kitchen gadget which makes showing it off more awkward. For prime showing off, objects must be happened upon inadvertently in the course of a relaxed and authentic soirée.

As in, 'You're right, Tiffanie. It isn't your imagination. We have got underfloor heating. James and I just felt that radiators were aesthetically problematic when we started renovating the oast.'

As in, 'Innocent Smoothies are all well and good, Tarquin, but we find there's never enough beetroot juice in them. Or acai berries. Or single-cell green algae. So we make our own.'

Whatever the reason, the Teasmade proved to be a fad.*

---

* Remarkably, the automated bedside tea-making device has made something of a comeback in the last three years. (So has the Sodastream but that's a whole different can of carbonated worms.) Swan

And then, like a fat kid on a seesaw, the microwave oven upset the fine balance between cutting corners and showing off. It was cheating, plain and simple. As the box with the magnetron and the strange magic powers took over kitchens of the eighties and we swapped proper cooking for the passing of non-ionising radiation through our food at a frequency of 2.45 gigahertz, it became clear that speed was more important than showing off.

This heralded a truly awful period in English culinary history, a wasteland with no messiah/Jamie Oliver to guide us through. Even Delia was largely off the telly in that gastro-vomique decade which explains why she had to teach us all to boil an egg again in 1998. It was the death of dinner-time, the serious maiming of breakfast and the grotesque Americanisation of our stomachs. Pop tarts. Microwave

---

Products is now manufacturing a modern Teasmade in China. You can buy it at John Lewis for £59.95. It is not gas-powered. It comes with an LCD alarm clock, a reading light and a rapid boil function which I don't understand the point of unless it's only there to make life easier for itself.

It looks very ergonomic – it would do well in a wind tunnel. I almost ordered one on the pretence of research and so I could tell you I'd got one and show off about it without having to invite you up to my bedroom, but then I read the reviews. Not so good. Some people loved it but aficionados comparing it to Ye Olde Teasmades were less compli-mentary. The light was too bright. It was too plasticky. It wasn't going to last for twenty years like our last one.

So I passed.

chips. A fork through some clingfilm, a ping and, 'Quick, we might still catch the start of *Blind Date*.'

We can blame almost everything on microwaves. Obesity, obviously. Mothers pushing those famous turkey twizzlers through school fences, indirectly. Divorce, probably. We mistook the microwave for freedom and it was really a magnotronic prison that locked up everything that was civilised about cooking.

ON THE OUTSKIRTS OF Windsor one Saturday morning, I knock on the door of a red-brick on one of those swirling cul-de-sacs and whisper to myself one last time, 'Be nice. She might be the chairman of all evil, but she's agreed to make you lunch.'

She answers. She looks friendly enough. But it's just a façade. Jennipher ('With a ph, it's a talking point') Marshall-Jenkinson is chairman of the Microwave Technologies Association. This organisation is brazen about its goals. Its aim? 'The education, training and dissemination of useful information for the end user of microwave ovens and microwave products.' This may as well read: 'the dissemination of useful information to push an already antisocial, unhealthy society into pierced-lid, stir-after-two-minutes, ping-based oblivion.'

'Hello,' I say, as cheerily as possible.

'Morning,' she replies with a smile.

Jennipher doesn't use a proper cooker. She does everything in a microwave. Or four microwaves, not counting the ones in the garage. She has raised two children entirely with microwave cooking and now she intends to subject me to a microwaved lunch. I should be angry on your behalf as well as my own but already the brainwashing has started. We're not having chips or tarts or, deep breath, a Feasters Flamegrilled Mega Burger Deluxe with Cheese (ninety seconds on high). We're having fresh salmon with mixed vegetables and new potatoes.

'You can't do potatoes in the microwave,' I say.

'You can,' she says, all evil.

'Isn't it healthier to steam vegetables?' I counter. 'At my house, we steam. If only everybody steamed everything rather than using microwaves, everything would be marvellous, wouldn't it?'

'You kill all the vitamin C when you steam,' she replies. 'You keep most of it if you microwave. If you boil vegetables, you lose up to 85 per cent of the nutrients. If you microwave them, you keep up to 85 per cent.'

One of the microwaves pings. The potatoes are done.

'Are your kids here?' I say because she can say what she likes about microwave cooking but it's meaningless without proof. Her microwave-raised progeny are bound to be spotty and podgy and below the average height. She steps away from her bank of microwaves to show me photographs of two strapping lads. One is a fitness instructor. The other looks perfectly fit as well. No obvious hunchbacks or withered limbs or radiated skin lesions.

Another microwave pings. The carrots in sesame and honey are done. Jennipher tells me some people can't cope with microwaved carrots because they taste too much like carrots. 'You're all used to the boiled, watery taste which is not what carrots actually taste like,' she says. How ridiculous. I can cope with her silly microwaved carrots.

Ping. Salmon. Ping. Mixed vegetables.

Twelve minutes after she started, Evil Jennipher has finished. The salmon is perfectly cooked, the new potatoes are delicious, the carrots . . .

My God, the carrots. They're just, well, very, very carroty. I mean, really, completely carrot-tasting. I find myself exclaiming at their sheer carrotiness. Worse, I find myself asking her why we don't all cook like this. It's so easy and quick and delicious and have I mentioned quick? And have I mentioned delicious? Jennipher sighs the sigh of a woman demonised by a society that refuses to accept the truth staring it in its belligerent, stupid face. It's quite a long sigh.

She explains that the microwave is only used for ready meals and nothing more creative and healthy because we are even more afraid of it than we were of pressure cookers. This might be true but it has also become a symbol of laziness. You would never use one at a pretentious dinner party. Can you imagine the sheer weight of pre-dinner drink disapproval if the only noise you could hear coming from the kitchen was the occasional ping? No whirr of a fancy cooker hood. Nothing.

Jennipher does microwave dinner parties. She does tomato soufflés, pesto garlic prawns, chicken liver pâté and monkfish on rosemary skewers. She even microwaves a Christmas lunch. This is obviously too much. I don't care how easy and quick and delicious a microwaved turkey might be, it's the definition of the end. What would Christmas be without the nine-hour wait by the oven for your *Tradition* (overcooked) turkey? But the rest sounds very convincing. When I leave this home of radiation cooking and carroty carrots, I will return to my family and inform them that the future is here. And it is called a microwave.

'What?' they will ask incredulously. 'From the eighties?' they will say.

'No,' I will reply. 'Behold a new type of microwaving. There will be no pre-packaged meals, my children. From henceforth, we shall eat fish and potatoes and carrots and we will be healthy and fit and good at sports, and we shall not be ashamed.'

IT LASTED A MONTH. I bought Jennipher's microwave cookbook and a load of microwave saucepans. We ate freshly prepared microwave meals and bored ourselves and everyone else with how healthy we were being. Then the novelty wore off. The Loyd Grossman pasta sauces and the Sloppy Giuseppes began whispering sweet nothings from their respective aisles. And then the sheer strain of remembering to buy carrots *and* honey *and* sesame seeds *and* salmon became too much. And I was back in the not-freshly prepared microwave meal aisle. And I was not alone. We spend more than £2 billion a year on ready meals. We consume twice as many as the French and five times as many as the Spanish. Throughout the recession, when we should all be eating offcuts and gruel, sales of ready meals have still continued to rise. The horsemeat scandal will only be a blip. What is wrong with us?

I'M AT THE END of an industrial estate on the outskirts of Derby in the midskirts of England putting on wellington boots, a white coat and a fetching green hair net. I wish I could tell you I'm here for a new and very niche dance night but, alas, I've come for a tour of S&A Foods, a company that employs 500 people to satisfy the insatiable ready-meal curry requirements of just one of the big four supermarkets. If the delicate relationship between showing off and cutting corners has been obliterated by the microwave, then it's not Jennipher's fault. It's the factories supplying the supermarkets supplying us, poor, defenceless, lazy us, with convenience food. Factories that might slip the odd horse into the lasagne mincer when we're not looking. Now, to be absolutely clear, S&A is a horse-free enterprise, but it is a huge cog in England's ready-meal machine.

My tour guide is Perween Warsi, the diminutive but determined chief executive, and immediately there is a problem. Perween is a foodie. She loves talking about food, cooking it, serving it. She's not very evil-factory-owner-forcing-us-to-eat-junk-food at all. In fact, we should probably be thanking her. Without her, we might all still be trapped in the 1970s. We might still think prawn cocktail crisps were the height of exotic sophistication.*

Perween arrived in Britain in 1975 armed with a rolling pin and a griddle, and found our cuisine woefully lacking. 'It was a very big shock coming from India where everyone spends all their time talking about food,' she explains. 'There was fish and chips with curry sauce, wrapped in newspaper, which was delicious but, you know, it was all really quite basic. Vegetables were stewed for hours. It was very hard to find good ingredients.'

Perween took one look at the samosas available in Dewsbury and started flogging her own. They sold like Teasmades and within weeks she had signed a contract with Asda to produce 5,000 meals a week. There were misgivings. Customers felt the masalas were too spicy. Buyers pleaded with her to ease off the spice. Perween refused. It was her mission to brighten our bland palates.

Nearly twenty-six years later, S&A Foods makes 1.5 million ready meals a week. 'And we stuck with proper spices. Our masala has won lots of awards. We even make a product called Scorching Hot Vindaloo.'

---

* Skips, as you will recall, first hit the shelves in 1974 and were an immediate success at cocktail parties the length and breadth of the Midlands.

I once spent a day at the factory that shreds the ice-berg lettuce you get in your Big Mac. I've never felt sorry for lettuce before. It is shredded at a rate of 1,000 kilo-grams an hour by a twenty-two-blade machine into which you wouldn't under any circumstances want to fall. It then drops onto a conveyor belt which propels it at four metres per second into a fluorolaser optical-sorting machine that cost the company a cool £350,000. The machine takes tens of thousands of scans a second to identify rogue chunks, grit and discoloration. In the unlikely event that a very hungry caterpillar had managed to make it past the shredder, this is where its adventure would end. When an anomaly is spotted, air guns blast the offending matter out of the flow. It is the lettuce equivalent of Ronald Reagan's Star Wars project.

Perween's factory is, of course, mechanised. Lots of big stainless-steel machines function very precisely to provide consistency, the be-all-and-end-all of mass-market pro-duction. The conveyor belt onto which robots are squirting sauce and chicken and rice is not exactly romantic. But it still feels very different from the Big Mac lettuce factory. The people making the sauce, marinating the chicken and boiling the rice are (a) not robots and (b) behaving exactly like chefs, albeit on a larger scale. Andaz, for example, is in the middle of cooking up a tikka. He isn't standing there operating a giant machine. He's standing there mixing ingredients in a wok the size of quite a posh paddling pool. It's industrial but still recognisably cooking. He's following a recipe: 104kg of onion, 0.4kg of cumin, 7kg of sugar, 7kg of tandoori paste and, well, I could go on but S&A would have to kill us. There are twenty-five ingredients, all chucked in and mixed by hand (or very large ladle).

In the rice-cooking department, Usman is cooking up a 100-kilogram batch.

'That's a lot of rice,' I say admiringly.

'No, it is small,' he says. 'We can do one and a half tonnes.' Usman is renowned as a bit of a rice wizard. He never burns it. He never overcooks it. He's a human rice robot.

The smell in the factory is quite distracting. It's hard to take notes as you peruse the racks of grilled vegetables and the vats of korma, madras and tikka. You can't ask Perween sensible questions because, frankly, you're just thinking about curry. Mmm, lovely curry. But this is just addiction, isn't it? We are addicted to ready meals and ready meals are bad for you both nutritionally and socially.

'There's been a huge change since we began,' says Perween when I ask if ready meals are evil. 'We had to redevelop our products with far less sugar, salt and fat. It's hard to do it. Salt is there for taste. Now we're almost at nil. It took a very long time to work out how to put the taste back.'

Even in the last decade, the English palate has changed. 'People have become much more knowledgeable and interested in food,' says Perween. 'They have therefore become influential. People want to understand what they're buying. A few years ago there was a fear that the young generation was losing their cooking skill. Delia Smith had to teach people to cook an egg. I couldn't believe it. Now, things are much better. There are so many cooking programmes and exotic food is part of the repertoire.'

As far as Perween is concerned, her ready meals have not destroyed that crucial family time in the kitchen. She thinks they've done the opposite. 'Women no longer want to be housewives and stay at home cooking every day. We are intelligent . . .'

'More intelligent than men.'

'Thank you. Women have less time for themselves and cooking takes a lot of your time. If I'm providing food that is already cooked, I am providing time for her to spend with her family.'

'Or watch Simon Cowell?'

'Is it the fault of ready meals or is it the fault of Simon Cowell?'

On the way home, I pop into Asda and buy a tikka (probably made by Andaz) with rice (probably boiled by Usman).

'I thought we were cooking fresh food in the microwave,' says Wife disapprovingly as I pierce the lid and prepare to wait the four long minutes for my curry to prepare itself. 'What happened to salmon and potatoes?'

'It's not the curry that's the problem. It's Simon Cowell.'

OUR LOVE OR, at the very least, my love of microwaved chicken tikka masala may continue unabated. Don't listen to the naysayers.* It's good for us, freeing up time to cope with our children's nightly interrogation on why centipedes don't have 100 legs, why fish don't die when lightning strikes water and why God took away our hamster. And it's not as if we don't eat it as part of a healthy, balanced diet, is it? You have your five a day, don't you? Of course you do. And it's not as if we don't use our microwaves as part of a balanced obsession with other gadgets.

In 2000, 171,000 of us bought breadmakers. In 2003 that figure more than trebled to 681,000. Today, spurred by the spiralling cost of supermarket-bought bread, it is estimated there could be as many as 10 million machines perched prettily on our kitchen surfaces. This is almost one for every other household. The breadmaker is the new Teasmade is the new pressure cooker and the entire nation should smell of that most delicious of smells, the smell that can attract estate agents from miles around, the smell of freshly baked bread. Except it doesn't. Ninety-five per cent of bread is still baked industrially and sold in plastic bags in supermarket aisles. How is this possible? It is possible because we are ridiculous. According to a Mintel survey in 2010, more than a third of breadmaking machines have *never been used*. It is

---

* Or, indeed, the neigh-sayers – if you did have a freezer stacked with Findus frozen lasagnes, it wouldn't have been the end of the world. Horse is perfectly nutritious. It is even a delicacy across Central Asia and Japan. And it was on the menu in Yorkshire until the 1930s.

England's least-used gift (sandwich toasters came second). Millions more have been used and then abandoned.

So not breadmakers after all. No, today's must-have kitchen gadget is the Celebrity Chef Cookbook. And before you say, 'But Delia's been around for decades,' she wasn't about showing off. As Perween points out, her *Complete Illustrated Cookery Course* begins with the section, 'What's an egg?' which is quite a long way away from the French complete cookery course, *Larousse Gastronomique*, which begins with a rather involved Beef Brandenburg and celery purée, and is bafflingly complicated throughout.

Now we have Gordon, Hugh, Heston and filthy Nigella. All peddling convenience and showing off. And we have Jamie, Britain's bestselling cookery author, king of short-cut showing off. He's made us a nation of olive-oil drizzlers, a nation au fait with crème fraîche, that just doesn't bother peeling our carrots because they look trendier that way. And the first recipe in his multi-platinum *30-Minute Meals* is not a boiled egg. It's broccoli orecchiette, courgette and bocconcini salad and prosciutto and melon drizzled with balsamic.

THERE'S SHOWING OFF and showing off. 'We are not so rarefied that we won't sell kitchens for £50,000 or £60,000. But it's not unusual for people to spend anything from £500,000 to £700,000 to even £1 million,' Robert Hughes, global sales director of kitchen-makers Clive Christian, told the *Daily Mail* in 2008 and, five years and one long recession later, they haven't exactly gone no-frills.

Standing by a nine-hob range in the Clive Christian showroom at the Chelsea Design Centre, it is abundantly clear how far our penchant for showing off can go if money isn't an issue.

'This is our cool luxury range,' says Carlos, the most discreet of salesmen, as he points out the chandeliers, the silver wood finish, the walnuts and hand-crafted architraving, the marble statues. It is an extraordinary sight to behold, half absolutely hideous, half stunning. You can easily imagine Roman Abramovich doing himself a toastie in here. 'We can personalise the furniture so you can have your initials or your family crest in the marquetry. Everything is handmade at the factory in Lancashire.'

Many of the Clive Christian clients have two kitchens; an industrial one for the staff and a nice, marble and wood one with statues and American fridges for entertaining. 'Or if the family decide to cook one night,' says Carlos.

It's like *Upstairs Downstairs* except everyone is in kitchens.

'The kitchen is the heart of the home. It used to be a separate room but now it's connected. We make sure all the rooms link together. It's very open plan.'

'How much would this kitchen cost?'

'About £100,000.'

'Oh,' I say, because I was hoping he might go a little higher.

'That's just for the furniture and wallpaper,' he says, sensing my disappointment. 'The appliances and the surfaces will be extra.'

The surfaces can cost tens of thousands. 'For us, it's the look,' says Carlos. 'We would recommend granite if the client wants to be practical. Marble will absorb water and show marks over time but it does really stand out.' Tough decision.

The cooker, if you go for La Cornue, which you must, darling, costs up to £24,000 and takes twelve weeks to deliver (so they have time to build your bespoke hob configuration). The taps . . . well, they're not going to be cheap either, are they? And then there's the Aquavision television behind the hob so you can watch the highlights of the Premiership football match you just scored a goal in. 'And you can connect it to the internet,' says Carlos.

Wow, I say. Because that really would put Mr Surrey's cooker hood in its place. 'It's the look, the feel, the lighting,' says Carlos. 'The first time you walk into a Clive Christian kitchen, you will be overwhelmed by the sheer luxury. I'll leave you to have a look around.'

Over by the entrance is another less cool, more blingy kitchen finished off with rose marbling and gold and silver cutlery. It's ex-display and it's going for half-price. Yours for £57,000. A couple walk in, browsing kitchens like you do. Carlos says hello and they say they're just looking.

'Just give me a shout if you need any help,' he says before retreating.

The couple start opening and closing cupboards in the half-price kitchen. The husband fiddles with a tap. The wife inspects the cutlery.

'It's £57,000,' he whispers. 'I can't believe people would pay that sort of money for a kitchen.'

'I know,' whispers the wife. 'But it would be good for showing off.'

TODAY, EVEN IF YOU HAVEN'T got a bargain £57,000 kitchen with an isthmus, a triple sink and a television behind the hob, even if your breadmaker is gathering dust and your range of celebrity cookbooks are as unused as the day someone unimaginative gave them to you for Christmas, even if your microwave knows nothing of sesame carrots and monkfish and everything of four-minute tikkas, this is a wonderful time for the English kitchen. It is where we have parties and coffee mornings using actual coffee machines, not Nescafé and sound effects. It is where we, occasionally,* do event-cheffing with foams and gelées and pan-fried scallops. And Sunday roast. They may take our lives but they will never take our Sunday roast.

In the twenty-first-century renaissance of the English kitchen, the relationship between showing off and cutting corners has taken on a new twist. Showing off is still in

* Okay, very occasionally. Okay, once. Jesus.

there but cutting corners? Sometimes we do, sometimes we gratuitously don't. It's a much more sophisticated balance than it was in the seventies. And I think we all know our way around a vegetable these days.

What's that, sorry? Morbid obesity? Type 2 diabetes epidemic? A rise in firefighters cutting Jabbas out of bath tubs? No, not listening. You're just being a spoilsport. The kitchen is the heart of the home, a happy, healthy heart. The sitting room, as we have established, is an offshoot, a place we go to because we are tired. So really, two chapters in, we're doing terribly well. But now we must step through the patio/conservatory/fully-receding-bringing-the-outside-in doors to the garden. And, good Lord, it's a jungle out there . . .

THE GARDEN

Gardening is cheaper than therapy and you get tomatoes.

Author unknown

THE DISPUTE BEGAN over a parking space shared between two homes in Cannock, Staffordshire, three years ago. On one side of the fence lived Mystic Ed, the 'celebrity psychic' and his civil partner Fluffy (aka Brian Murphy). They liked to play Christmas carols all year round and had a very large, very bronze floodlit statue of Michelangelo's *David* in their garden. On the other side of the fence lived Bill Podmore, an altogether less flamboyant individual, who claimed the enthusiastic carol concerts would sometimes keep him awake until half-three in the morning. His garden had fewer floodlit *David*s (i.e. none) and more discarded lawnmowers and television sets. Even if there had been no parking dispute, it's safe to say he was never going to be best friends with Mystic Ed and Fluffy.

The argument over the parking space escalated. The tutting and curtain-twitching developed into fracas, name-calling and an incident in which one party lay on the other party's front lawn. The police, the magistrate's court and the council all became involved.

'It is putting years on me,' Mystic Ed told his local newspaper last summer. 'I may look all right, but that's down to what you can get out of a tube. Deep within myself I want to run off.'

'They're being unreasonable,' Podmore responded. 'They're both useless and one's head is too big.'

A council spokesman said, 'We are aware of the ongoing issues.'

Ongoing issues. A phrase that sums up so many relationships with neighbours. Meanwhile, in a quiet and entirely uneventful cul-de-sac in deepest Tufnell Park, a different set of issues was ongoing. It started thirty years ago when the new family arrived across the fence. All smiles, handshakes, welcomes to the neighbourhood, no problems whatsoever with the shared parking space or the footballs that, from time to time, came over the fence and would, at some point, I'm telling you, darling, break a pane of glass in the greenhouse (but never have). The new arrivals were British Bangladeshi which, quite frankly, the cul-de-sac needed. A bit of foreign culture to brighten up the once-a-decade street parties. All was well and good.

But then, on day three, the gobbing started. At four forty-five each morning, the patriarch of the new household would step out onto his lawn, consider his existence, his place in the grand scheme of things and his plan for the day, and then he would hack up a knotty, semi-viscous greenie like a cat hacks up a fur ball.

Thirty years ago, Bert Across the Fence, slept with the back bedroom window open and set his alarm for seven each morning. This still left plenty of time to ablute, to dress, to get to work on his bike. But after the hacked greenie on days three, four, five, eight (they went away for the weekend), nine, ten and eleven, he found himself waking up in antici-pation at four forty. Then four thirty. Then four. He tried sleeping with the window shut but the more muffled the hacking, the more extensively he woke up to listen out for it. He tried earplugs, sleeping pills and pillows. But now his ear was fine-tuned to it. He could pick it out through any amount of medicinal or physical muffling.

For the first ten years, he wondered if he should say something. He didn't want to offend but really, this was no way to live. Every time he resolved to bring up the bringing up, his resolution dissolved on final approach. This was his neighbour. This was his neighbour's phlegm. It was simply too intimate to mention. Year eleven, he started getting up and going downstairs at four forty. By four forty-five, he was in the kitchen making tea. Ten years later, newly retired, no longer needing to wake up for anything at all except the twice-monthly film club, Bert moved into the other bedroom, the small one with the poor view, the one nowhere near his neighbour's garden. It was too late. Thirty years on from the first fur ball, Bert still gets up at four forty. Ongoing issues.

Then there's the man who spent a day in prison after urinating on his neighbour's hedge for a year. And the couple who got sent down for a fortnight because they took a chainsaw to a hawthorn. And another couple fighting a £100,000-and-counting court battle over a twelve-inch boundary disagreement. All ongoing issues. That terrifying little phrase. You could argue that Mystic Ed should have seen his issues coming. He is psychic, after all. But everywhere else across the land, there is sniping, nit-picking, gossiping, bad-mouthing, setting of bear traps. And at its extreme, there are full-on wars: hydrangea wars, shed wars, treehouse wars and, of course, cypress leylandii wars. What is the catalyst that makes otherwise reserved, polite, reasonable, even friendly English people waste thousands in litigation? Or worse, get locked up? Or worse still, commit murder? Because of a hedge?

If an Englishman's home is his castle, then an Englishman's hedge is his moat. And the cypress leylandii is the biggest, nastiest moat of all. You remember how, in the movie *Arachnophobia*, the massive Venezuelan killer spider sneaks into a wooden box, flies to the small town of Canaima, USA, and mates with house spiders to create a new super-species of evil killer spiders that threaten to take over the entire town? Very similar story with the cypress leylandii. In the 1840s the Liverpudlian banker Christopher

Leyland (it would be a banker) bought Leighton Hall, Powys, and gave it to his nouveau riche cousin as a wedding present. The cousin splashed £275,000 (£24 million in today's money) on having the whole thing rebuilt in the Gothic style, complete with bling garden too.

This was in the days before Jacuzzis, tantric yoga pavilions and infinity pools so the cousin did his bling with flora exotica. In one section, he planted Monterey cypress, a Californian conifer renowned for its fast growth but not particularly hardy. In another section a few hundred yards away, he planted Nootka cypress, an Alaskan conifer renowned for its resilience, but slow-growing. In the wild, these two species had always been kept at a safe distance. But one steamy night in the 1880s, the two trees had sex, and, with an evil crack of thunder, the leylandii was conceived. It took the fast-growing bit from the Monterey and the well-hardness from the Nootka, and now, just 130 years later, it has taken over England and sent us all mad. Right now, there are approximately 17,000 neighbours at loggerheads (snigger) over the illegitimate offspring of those two naughty trees.

You would think, given that it doesn't support wildlife, that it sucks life from everything around it, that it needs pruning not once, not twice but three times a year to keep it from BLOCKING OUT THE SKY, that it might not have caught on. That our already complicated set of social interactions with neighbours did not need a bloody great hedge chucked in. But that would be to underestimate the Englishman's intense need for privacy. Privet doesn't do privacy like the Leyland cypress – and nor does buxus.

'BEWARE OF THE DOG,' says an angry sign in the window but, frankly, that's the least of my worries. As I wait for the door to be answered, I am bracing for the worst. You can do this, Matt. Just maintain eye contact and you'll be fine.

'Allo,' says Leslie, which is only one notch down from 'Ayup'.

Thank God, I think. Leslie is wearing clothes. I have driven all the way to Keighley, West Yorkshire, wondering if I'll have to interview the seventy-something-year-old in the buff because Leslie needs privacy more than most. He is a naturist. Has been for fifty years.

'I was in my twenties and I wanted to stop smoking,' he says. 'I decided I'd go to a naturist club because then I wouldn't have any pockets.'

'Seriously?'

'Spielplatz Naturist Club, just this side of London. I drove down the first weekend, sat in the car in the lane outside for fifteen minutes and then drove away. I did that three weekends in a row. On the third weekend, I was sat in the lane and a car came up behind me. Beep, beep, beep. So I drove up to the main gates to turn around and this woman came out with nothing on and asked if she could help. Haven't looked back since.'

'Did you stop smoking?'

'No.'

I'm sitting in his dining room, admiring his professional karaoke set, trying not to admire the naturist calendar on the wall. (Leslie was Mr January – he did it for a cancer charity. I don't ask if it made any money.) Besides being an eccentric in the best sense of the word, Leslie is a rare example of someone who has been in dispute about his leylandii but settled it without any real argument or fight or attempted strangulation. There were special circumstances.

'The neighbours came round and asked me to get rid of it,' he says. 'I told them I liked to be naked in the garden and they decided the hedge could stay. We get on great now but I do feel bad that the hedge blocks light into their kitchen.'

'It's there because it's thick. It's a horrible bloody thing really. A nasty tree. For me, it's about privacy but a lot of people use it as a weapon, just to upset the neighbours.'

Why though, Leslie? Why?

'People are territorial,' he says. 'We've been under-privileged in the past. We've always been the serfs. Now we've got our bit of land. We've got leisure time. We like to potter.'

'You're a potterer?'

'No, but English people these days can potter. They do potter. I was born in Liverpool in 1940. Back then, any bit of land had vegetables grown on it. Them days, you had nothing. No land. A bit of yard and that was it. And there wasn't any leisure time.'

Now, Leslie finds himself in another fight, a fight that sums up everything about local councils, territory, hedges and an Englishman's God-given right to strip off in his own garden if he bloody well likes. This particular fight is not with the neighbour but with future neighbours. The council has sold a thin patch of land on the other side of Leslie's house. Developers want to squeeze three new homes onto it. It's difficult to see where but they'll manage. They always do.

'I phoned the council up and asked what happens when they've built the houses and people look out the window and they see me with nowt on. They said they'll phone the police and I'll be charged with indecent exposure. But they can't. The only way they can do that is if they can prove I was walking around in a lewd manner.'

'How do you walk in a lewd manner? Is it saucy walking?'

'A seventy-year-old? Don't be ridiculous. What are they going to do?'

'I wonder if they'll list you in the estate agent's details? Warning: naturist.'

'I doubt it. We're very prudish in this country. People will go to Rome and there's bloody statues of naked fellows there, and they'll say, "Oh, look at that, that's a work of art." No, that's a bit of stone. The bloody human body's a work of bloody art.'

Leslie is not a radical naturist. You won't see him rambling the Three Peaks in the nude. Or wandering down your high street in the buff. 'Not everyone wants to see a man stark bollock naked,' he says. 'If the doorbell goes, I'll wrap myself in a towel' (although he has been known to see off persistent Jehovah's Witnesses with the threat of a towel-free greeting).

'I'm not really bothered about my line in the sand. I just don't want to embarrass anybody.'

'So what will you do when the houses go up?'

'I'm just going to carry on doing what I'm doing. We don't get enough sunshine in Yorkshire so when we do get it, why cover yourself up with clothes? Everyone round here knows, especially the women: if they want to have a go, they're always welcome in my garden.'

Right. I'll pass that on. With a warm handshake and a promise to give stripping a go in my own back garden, I leave him and his 'ongoing issues', thinking, he isn't asking much. Privacy. A small patch of England to call his own. That's all he wants.

IT'S NOT ALL EVERYONE WANTS, not if the frenzied hordes rushing around the Hampton Court Flower Show this particular Saturday are anything to go by. No. Apparently people who aren't Leslie want pagodas and Tahitian al fresco dining areas and handcrafted shepherd's huts too. I had planned to find out what the very latest things going on in the English garden might be so I could tell you and we could all be very horticulturally à la mode but I've been caught up in the frenzy. It's not even half-ten and I've more or less decided I can't live without many garden ornaments and a very flash gazebo. I'm not the only one.

Trapped in a wooden pavilion like slugs in a salt factory or Lottery winners at this very flower shower, a large, sunburnt couple are being given the pitch for a £19,000 'leisure building'. It is a hell of a leisure building, bigger than most people's gardens and sold complete with a twelve-seat dining table and a huge flat-screen television that appears only to show Elton John concerts. Which would obviously be brilliant. As I always say, you can never have enough Elton. The roof (of the pavilion, not Elton) is thatched in the Polynesian style and guaranteed for thirty years, and really, says the saleswoman, working her Out-of-Africa-into-Hunter-wellies look very hard indeed, 'you can do pretty much anything with the interior'.

'This brochure should give you some inspiration,' she says, reminding them that that £19,000 is a special show price and anyway, look how sunburnt they are. They must need somewhere to shelter. And then she wanders off, leaving them to that hushed, furious argument sunburnt couples have when only one of them wants to spend £19,000 on a shed and the other one just thought they were here for a nice day out.

Sheds are obviously the thing at this year's show. Traditionally the last retreat of the exhausted, bullied, henpecked, depressed, washed-up, washed-out, passed-over middle-aged family man, they have become the garden equivalent of a DFS white leather sofa suite with cuddler and motorised recliner.

Bespoke shepherd's hut makers Court and Hunt sold three of their stylish £11,000 models yesterday and have had many more 'serious enquiries'. They've also watched as someone purchased the entire show garden opposite them for £8,000, plants, trees, water features, urns, shed, the lot – saves time and the use of your own imagination, I suppose. A few rows along, a company called My Place in the Garden has already sold two of their 'places in the garden' this morning which, they tell me, could be a music room, an art studio, a hobby room, a pottery studio or even a writer's haven.*

'Not just a shed in which a grown man can drink supermarket cider and have a little cry, then?'

'No.' For a moment, I'm tempted. It's about time I started a new hobby. Pottery might be just the thing. Or matchstick modelling. Our current shed is full of junk so if I got a bigger shed, I could do pottery/modelling and have enough storage space to store all the things that need storing without having to chuck things on top of things so I can never find things. This is the only possible explanation for how anyone could turn up to a flower show and spend thousands and thousands of pounds on what is still a shed. An impulse shed purchase.

As I reach for my credit card, I am distracted by the Stainless Steel Barbecue Company. We needn't get overexcited

---

* Note to My Place in the Garden: writers don't have havens, they have holes, hovels and isolated hotels. Redrum. Redrum. Redrum.

about barbecues in this chapter. Despite the Englishman's basic instinct to um make um fire, burning food outside still isn't culturally significant the way it is in Australia or South Africa. Nevertheless, can we pause for a moment to behold the Ultimate Ikon BBQ, a hand-forged, stainless-steel, life-guaranteed behemoth of a thing, yours for just £1,600 ('special show price'). Above the main charcoal pit, various grills and griddles move into and out of the heat as chef (or you, the man in the apron with the wife who isn't talking to you because you spent £1,600 on a barbecue, you idiot) requires. In addition to the many cooking areas, there is room for pre-cooked meat, room for post-cooked/ burnt meat, room for your chilled bottle of Chablis/Bishop's Finger/home-made sloe gin and your Pringles/Kettle chips/ home-made pork scratchings. Non-ultimate barbecues never cater for these sorts of things. You have to balance stuff on the wall or the lid of the barbecue. It's so . . . unseemly. But the Ultimate is a thing of beauty, a gentle yet powerful assertion of masculinity like that Arena poster. It is the barbecue equivalent of running off with the secretary or thinking you might buy a vintage Porsche while at the same time completely understanding that you are not getting any younger. The Ultimate Ikon Penis Extension.

I phone home.

She says no, don't be bloody ridiculous.

In the Floral Marquee, a polytunnel the length of the Eurotunnel full of beautiful, improbable plants, hundreds of gardeners and wannabe gardeners are stretching their imaginations. Culture-shocked bonsais, temperamental ferns, shivering figs and high-maintenance orchids are all being carted off by wildly optimistic new owners. If plants could speak (which they can't, Your Royal Highness), they wouldn't be speaking. They'd be screaming, ''elp! Cristiano, 'elp! I'm being taken by zis man who az only ever grown zee daffodil and zee runner bean! 'elp!' In a South American accent, obviously. Because they're from the Amazon.

In the Rose Tent, a decidedly less exotic marquee, sellers are trying to keep calm before tomorrow's storm. Tomorrow is the last day. From five o'clock, all hell will break loose as the display flowers are sold for cheap.

'I'll give you a fiver for it,' they'll say.

'No.'

'A tenner then?'

'No.'

'People will climb up these trellises to get at those hanging baskets,' says the veteran nurserywoman pointing high up at the ceiling, breathing into a paper bag in anticipation. 'They go crazy.'

I'm not that bad, I think, back at home, mowing the lawn using string for precision stripes.* For example, right off the top of my head, I haven't got a ride-on lawn mower, the mobility scooter of gardening. I bought the Bosch Rotak 40

---

* Sorry, lying. I don't use string. I use a laser pen. Nope, that's not true. I'm totally relaxed about lawn-stripe straightness (see next three pages).

thirteen-inch rear-roller Ergoflex Cordless Mower because a petrol one was prohibited by the Rudd Family Save the Polar Bears Committee but cordlessness in all things is what Englishmen should aspire to most in life.

Of course, the Rotak 40's battery runs out if I don't mow the lawn at a steady jog, which takes some of the fun out of it. I can't really stop for minor obstructions like children's toys, slugs or Wife's newly deployed bedding plants. And I've had to learn to turn ends like an Olympic swimmer. And the neighbour has a petrol mower and rubs it in my face. But the grass is always greener on the other side, isn't it? I'm not going to start urinating on his cypress leylandii about it.

The more taxing issue is lawn stripes. Instinctively, I know they are terribly suburban, the preserve of people who enjoy pointless order in their lives, who understand the merits of waxing a car, who alphabetise their bookshelves and iron their Y-fronts. One quick skim of the various online gardening forums confirms this. There are countless (well, seven) people bemoaning the fact that they bought a certain type of Flymo that doesn't do stripes 'like on football pitches'. All (seven) of them live in Bracknell.

But I do like a stripe. I consulted a psychologist who said it was part of the national psyche, a need to impose order on chaos, to make nature conform, a colonial hangover even. We want nature but we want it to be not very natural. It comes from the same part of the brain that makes Englishmen wear socks and sandals. We want to enjoy the beach, but we don't want sand between our toes. That would be too much. Psychologists can read too much into things. It might just be because sand between your toes is horrible.

My love of lawn stripes does know several bounds. For example, I won't move the trampoline or the garden table to maintain the integrity of a stripe. Not every week anyway. I will mow around and under them in a non-linear way which is, as I'm sure you will agree, devil-may-care. It is true that the little tufts of unreachable grass annoy me for most of the intervening week, even when I'm not in the garden, even when I'm trying to go to sleep and I can sense the deformity, sense it laughing at me, laughing, I tell you, but the point is, they are there. I am no lawn anorak. Also, I sometimes mow a diagonal strip right across the lawn at the end to get to the compost heap. Okay?

For another example, also totally off the top of my head, I haven't got a leaf-blower. I will never get a leaf-blower. A leaf-blower is worse than a 1,000-foot-high cypress leylandii. Like so many destroyers of all that is civilised (e.g. Happy Meals, the Kardashian sisters, the expressions, 'You do the math', 'I'm reaching out to you', and 'Happy Holiday!'), we inherited the concept of blowing leaves from the Americas and we have run with it. In twenty-first-century England, you know when it's autumn because the air sharpens, the geese fly south, the sun shines bright but cool and the lazy tranquillity of the season is murdered by the noise of a million idiots blowing leaves from one end of the garden to the other. In particular, I know when it's autumn because every Sunday I watch a thin, hunched, angular, lizard-eyed sixty-year-old hoodlum blow his leaves down his drive, stop, look up and down the road to check the coast is clear and then blow the lot onto the pavement. Which isn't his.

Bored, I once asked Bosch to explain the point of this invention. 'Leaf-blowers propel air from their nozzles with the purpose of moving garden debris such as leaves and twigs to make it easier to tidy and organise the garden,' they said, rather literally. 'They prevent the need to spend long periods of time sweeping.'

Ridiculous. Two-thirds of the way through a ninety-page report on Californian leaf-blowers (excellent bedtime reading), an academic cites a study that found a link between background noise and a human's willingness to help a fellow human. This has actually been tested. If you drop your shopping near a noisy construction site, people are less likely to help you pick it up than if you dropped it on a quiet country lane. This is not because country folk are nicer. It's because of the noise. Even the background hum of a (petrol) lawnmower makes people less helpful. Leaf-blowers are louder. If we could all go back to rakes, the world would be a nicer place. But we can't go back.

OVER THE LAST CENTURY, the role of the garden has changed dramatically. Before the Second World War, the average home had a front room, a dining room, a small kitchen and a yard or, if you were lucky, a garden. Maybe with some grass. Now, the house has been flipped around. The front room looking onto the street has become the big kitchen-diner looking out onto the garden. The sitting room at the front is for watching telly, not for entertaining. Accordingly, the garden has had to pull up its socks. It is no longer a place to shove the bike, the outhouse loo, the washing line and the vegetable patch. In estate agent's parlance, it has become a room outside.

Pessimists might projectile vomit as they link this to the decline of community. Looking away from the street rather than out to it is wrong. Neighbourhood is not watched. Optimists suggest this marks the rise of the modern English family – insular, yes, but sharing each other's lives around the kitchen table, the damned television and, weather permitting, leaf-blower permitting, the garden.

'We are a creative nation,' says Colin Crosbie, curator at Wisley, flagship garden of the Royal Horticultural Society, as he plucks one of the very few weeds from an otherwise perfect rose garden.

'We're so good at putting ourselves down but how many things does England lead the way in?' Silence. I look at my feet. A group of Japanese tourists walk past, pointing at a herbaceous border. 'Okay, maybe not the football or the rugby—'

'Or the cricket any more.'

'Or the cricket any more. Thank you. But when it comes

to horticulture, to gardening, on whatever level, we lead the world. Look at that lovely, bright alstroemeria . . .'

And he's off again, marching, sallying forth, a man with David Bellamy's enthusiasm and Billy Connolly's sing-song Scottish accent.

'English people love garden centres. Where else in the world would a day out constitute going to a garden centre? It's a family day out. Gardens are getting smaller and smaller – but they've become far more important. You look at what people will pay for mantelpiece ornaments and LED tellies and nice, new sofas. Well, they want their garden to be like that as well.'

Left turn, right turn, into another corridor of bloom.

'The typical English garden used to be a rectangle of striped lawn with flowerbeds around the side but now it's very hard to define what is typical. The garden gives people a chance to express themselves. Do they have brightly coloured borders or do they go natural with a few bird feeders? It's a journey. No one can tell you what's right and wrong.'

Right turn, left turn, past a woman with an umbrella and a child chasing a butterfly.

His own garden, where he goes to unwind each evening after a stressful day running a garden, is full of blues and whites (he doesn't like anything bright red or variegated – they don't look natural). He also has a vegetable patch which, when his boys were younger, provided the staples but has become more adventurous and exotic as they've grown older.

'That's the thing about gardens,' he says, in a way that makes you want to run off and do some weeding, leaving him mid-sentence, mid-tour. 'They're always changing. When you buy a picture and hang it on the wall, that's it. But plants never stay the same.'

A century ago, Wisley had 5,000 visitors a year. Now it has one million. 'We were quite an elitist place but now we're for everyone,' says Crosbie. 'You used to need money to garden. Now, people garden in a window box. Something has changed. We want to compete with the neighbours, keep up with the Joneses. Yes, there's that element of competition but also of pride. Ownership. People are proud of their street, their town, their park and, most importantly, their garden. That's coming back again.'

Crosbie is an evangelist. If he was preaching religion, he'd be living on an island with a whole bunch of apostles and several hundred litres of cyanide-laced lemonade. Fortunately, he picked gardening. As intoxicating as he makes it all sound, it's still hard to believe that the English are really that green-fingered. Beyond the odd burst of pottering, the occasional foray to Homebase, surely the 800 television channels and Wii and iPlayer and seasons one to five of *Breaking Bad* suck up the spare time like those three rubbish television channels never could in the seventies? In the age of entertainment, not to mention subprime belt-tightening, you would expect the garden might be the first thing to be neglected.

'It's not like that,' says Crosbie, as we reach Wisley's shop.

'We go to work. We come back. We sit. We watch the telly. We look at the computer screen. If that's all we do, we're just going to end up like creatures in a zoo. Why do people still want to go cycling, to go walking at weekends, to garden? It's because we have to get out. We must.'

The shop is full of people pushing trolleys around like they're on *Supermarket Sweep*. Some of them look just like the cyber-family from Chapter One. I'm sure they all have a thousand iPads and they can slouch on a sofa like the best of them but right now they're hell-bent on recreating their own mini-Wisleys.

GLADSTONE STREET, Wigston, Leicestershire. Not a very exciting street, a terraced cul-de-sac just round the corner from a car dealership and a McDonald's. Things Wigston has going for it: it's five minutes from Leicester by train and it is home to the Wigston Framework Knitters Museum. Sadly, the museum is only open from two until five on Sundays and today is Saturday. Unsadly, I'm not here for the knitting. I'm here to snoop around Chris and Janet Huscroft's garden. They are not naturists and they don't have a big hedge. Other than that, I know nothing. I've never met them before and I'm just turning up, completely unannounced, in the driving rain to have a look around.

'Hello, I've come to look around your garden.'

'Right. Lovely,' says Janet. 'Chris is in the greenhouse. I'll get him.'

This is quite weird, quite unEnglish. Who, in their right mind, would let a complete stranger have a nose round their garden? Show-offs, perhaps.

'Thanks very much,' I reply, as she leads me down the side passage, over a little decorative bridge to Chris who is, as advertised, in his greenhouse. He doesn't seem like a show-off. He's a gentle man, unassuming, retired at sixty-two with 'many, many interests'.

The Huscrofts, along with 4,000 other householders, are part of the National Garden Scheme. They charge a small fee to let you look round their garden. The fee goes to charity. It's the National Trust minus the fudge, the grandeur, the folding picnic chairs, the vaguely sinister room attendants (ask me about the room, heathens), the tomato soup, the tea cosies, the craft walking sticks and the historic tales of inbreeding, suicide, bad portraiture and privilege.

The garden I have driven 145 miles to see is sixty-three feet long by fifteen feet wide, a terrace rectangle that ordinarily would not be worth the journey. But look what they've done. Look what they've only gone and done. Past the lawn ('which takes two minutes to mow'), over the bridge and you're 'in another world', as Chris puts it only about 4 per cent over-optimistically. On one side is a wood-land glade, on the other side a more Mediterranean vibe. It's an abundant jungle of mismatched planting, chaotic and ordered at the same time. Past the greenhouse, under a thick canopy of trees, there is a 'shade house' full of rare ferns, hostas and arisaemas. In the space most of us would manage a clothes line, a patch of striped lawn and a rusty barbecue ('Why didn't you put it in the shed before winter like I said, darling?'), Chris and Janet have created a small Eden.

'We've been here forty years but the garden has evolved over the decades,' says Chris. 'You don't have to stick to the rules any more. Years ago, people would never mix roses and herbaceous borders but there's been an evolution of informality. This informality suits us. We can put almost any plant in here and it won't look out of place. We don't colour coordinate or anything like that. We buy what we like and it has to be shoehorned in somewhere.'

'Do you argue over which plants you put where?' I ask, looking for some holes in this paradise.

'We have never had any arguments whatsoever,' he says adamantly, reminding me ever so slightly of Bill Clinton. 'We discuss everything.'

'But why do you let strange people like me in? Is it showing off?'

'We can't show off with a little terrace house and such a small garden, can we?' says Janet.

'I love our garden and my wife loves our garden,' says Chris. 'We're more than happy to share it with other people. Because we love it so much, we feel we want to share it. There's such a sense of excitement. What will people think?'

'But they're strangers? Who cares what they think?'

'They're not strangers. Gardeners are like one big bunch of friends. It's such a leveller. It's like the weather. The

English are great talkers about gardens and weather. You turned up today and we spent the first ten minutes talking about the weather. It broke the ice and now we're talking about all sorts of things.'

This is confusing. Gardens as social epicentres rather than battlegrounds. The hedge wars are just an extreme, an anomaly, another media exaggeration. According to Wisley Colin and Wigston Janet and Chris, the English garden is a far more positive place, a refuge, an antidote to our iLives.

WHEN I WAS THIRTEEN, I got an allotment but I got it for all the wrong reasons. I was a Thatcher's child. I reasoned that I could grow vegetables and flog them and make a killing. With the encouragement of all the old duffers and the feigned enthusiasm of my family, I stuck it out for five years.

'More sugar beet, son? How simply marvellous.'

I never made a penny but I did experience the Zen-like calm that comes with digging couch grass and turning potatoes. I also glimpsed the dream of self-sufficiency before abandoning it all for (some) beer and (not enough) women and a (sort-of) career.

In 1988 waiting lists for allotments were unheard of. Whole sections of my allotment grounds lay abandoned to nettles and brambles. The council was itching to get its hands on the 'prime real estate' and magic it into yet another housing estate. These days, the council is still itching but my old allotments have become the heart of the community. Every last inch is cultivated. There are open days where the general public can come in just to look at other people's vegetables. And if you want to join the cult of grow-your-own, you must join a two-year waiting list. This is true across the country. On average, for every one person digging spuds on an allotment in England, there is another person waiting to dig spuds.

And we've diversified. In my day (I've always wanted to say that), we grew runner beans, beetroot, potatoes and, if I were lucky, courgettes. One season, I planted some squash and it made the local newspaper. Now, you'll find aubergine, fennel, rocket and sage, chicory, artichoke and garlic. It's all very Duchy Original.

Imagine what England's best allotment must be like.

Imagine no longer. I'm standing in the middle of it.

'Don't stand there, you're on the radishes,' says Antonio.

'Sorry.'

'Don't mind him,' says Mary. 'He's like that.'

Antonio and Mary have won *Garden News*'s Allotment of the Year competition not once but twice, two years in a row. This means a lot to Antonio who arrived from Italy more than half a century ago and has tended his prize allotment at the back of a housing estate in Crawley for forty years. He is eighty-two but he looks about sixty which, for the purposes of this book, we will be attributing entirely to his vegetable-growing endeavours. Mary looks a tiny little bit older than sixty and is a little younger than eighty but she has to live with Antonio and Antonio is a perfectionist.

'I like things to be right,' says Antonio.

The couple start at seven in the morning, getting a couple of hours of allotmenting out of the way before breakfast. They come back mid-afternoon for a three-hour session and Antonio will sometimes return in the evenings. Because vegetables don't grow themselves. Or as Antonio puts it, 'Good fortune doesn't fall out of the sky.'

The result is something to behold and beholding it is not optional. In terms of enthusiasm, Antonio makes the carpet sellers of downtown Kahramanmaras look laid back. He takes me by the elbow or the shoulder or the scrunch of shirt: 'Come see this, come see this, look, you see beautiful courgette, I give you good price.' Except his produce is not for sale. He can't even pick it right now (the next judging panel arrives in three weeks). We can only look at his potatoes. And his tomatoes. And his lettuce, endive, garlic, courgette, cauliflower, cabbage, aubergine, fennel, onion, leek, beans (French, haricot, borlotti, broad, runner), carrots, peas, artichoke, rocket, pumpkin, cucumber, chard, broccoli, celery, corn, radish, eleven types of herb, four varieties of apple, four varieties of fig ('Avoid the Turkish ones – they don't grow well here'), plum, thornless blackberry, blueberry, raspberry, strawberry, mulberry, quince, grape and goji berry. Totally down with his superfoods.

Antonio and Mary's allotment is the equivalent of the super-striped lawn. There are no weeds. None. Weeds fear this place. In their stead, there are perfectly straight lines of perfectly tended vegetables. Towards the back, the avenue of fig, grape and olive puts you in mind of an Umbrian hilltop villa. Antonio makes his own wine. He distributes surplus crops to friends, neighbours, the local hospice. It is another Eden. Almost.

When Antonio first took his allotment, the site was half empty. Now, fifty people are on the waiting list. And yet several patches are distinctly undermanaged. 'Do you call that an allotment?' says Antonio, genuinely annoyed at a neighbouring plot specialising in brambles.

'Look at that one,' says Mary. 'They've got strawberries there *and* strawberries there. And that's it.'

'This one was given warnings,' says Antonio, warming to his theme. 'He comes down, scratches around a little bit, and then, puff, gone again for six months. People go mad in the first year. Next year, they're gone.'

Poor Antonio. Poor Mary. All they want is for the others to appreciate the importance of the allotments, to maintain basic standards.

'I will look at what people have done, and I will tell them it is not quite right,' he says, and I'm suddenly feeling less sorry for him. 'A bit of advice, you know. I'm afraid some of them can be a little bit stubborn. They can resent it. I'm soft at first but if you persist in not trying hard enough, I will get angry.'

Antonio is the strong-willed minor character in *Midsomer Murders*, the one with the cast-iron alibi you still can't quite stop suspecting. Some of his fellow gardeners bug him and, I'm guessing, he bugs some of them. He's caught the English disease. No, not that one. The one where the symptoms are manifested as raised eyebrows and audible muttering. He's not Mystic Ed. It's not that bad by miles. But he's Jones and he wants the Smiths to keep up.

The English garden, whether it's an improbable Eden on the outskirts of Leicester, a pristine allotment under the Gatwick flight path or a leylandii-enclosed naturist's paradise, is not just about territory or even privacy. It's a place of order and refuge in a chaotic world. The shed – from the humble 4x3 right up to the Hampton Court Tahitian roundhouse – is merely an extension of that. We all want a place where we can just do our thing, even if our thing is to measure our lawn stripes, rearrange pots or argue interminably about the best way to light a barbecue. This is why you have hedge wars and it's why leaf-blowers are Satan's whoopee cushions. Anything that intrudes upon this small piece of tranquillity will be met with ultimate force. Or, in the case of the phlegmatic morning chorus, an audible tut.

'Are you going to retire at some point?' I ask Antonio as I prepare to leave.

'Never,' he replies.

'He never will,' agrees Mary admiringly.

'You know where you're born but you don't know where you're going to die,' he explains, before insisting I inspect a new variety of endive.

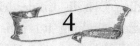

THE COMMUTER TRAIN

We kissed at the barrier; and passing through
She left me, and moment by moment got
Smaller and smaller, until to my view
She was but a spot.

THOMAS HARDY, commuter

SEVENOAKS STATION, KENT. Five twenty-five on a Monday morning and not only have I not kissed her at the barrier, I have not kissed her at home either. Obviously, she was asleep (still with a pillow on her head). And it's drizzling. It would be all right if it was raining. When it rains, we know where we stand even if it's in a puddle right up to our middle. Umbrellas. Wet trouser legs. Soup for lunch. You can sing in the rain, tap dance in it, twirl your umbrella in it. You can run through it in your boxers for a dare. Or if you're too old and you only have the M&S Y-fronts your wife buys you in packs of five (excellent value,

95

good testicular support), you can look up into the broiling skies, put a hand out and say, 'At least it's good for the plants,' before wandering off to your allotment. It's drizzling though. Just drizzling. Drizzle, drizzle, drizzle. You can't do anything with drizzle. Nothing. It is generated, as you will know if you are English, by stratocumulus clouds which are easily the dullest of all clouds and because it falls in droplets of less than half a millimetre in diameter, you hardly even notice it's there. Like Basingstoke or your own mortality. A lurking presence, intangible but incrementally depressing. Damp.

Even without the drizzle, five twenty-five is a horrible time of day unless you're en route to an airport to catch a flight to Nice or Aruba or Phuket or you're holding your three-month-old, smiling baby after the first six-hour sleep straight through or you're still up partying the day after you realised you'd won £165 million on the Lottery and you don't have to live in the wrong bit of Ayrshire any more. Today, none of these things has happened. It's just drizzling.

Still, I am awake for an experiment. I'm testing miserableness, because miserableness is what the English are famous for. Complaining. Moaning. Whingeing. Not looking on the bright side. Miserableness. It's what we do best. And where is the place you will find miserableness in its most concentrated form? On a train platform at half-five in the morning. I'm not even here to get a train and I'm miserable. Just look how long I went on about the drizzle. For the subjects of my experiment, the commuters, the miserableness count will be high. The train platform on Monday morning is as far as you can get from the refuge of the sofa, the warm glow of the kitchen, the calm and order of the garden. It is the start of the working week, waiting for the train that will take you away from your home and into the maelstrom of work. It will be almost unbearable to witness.

I'm standing in a kiosk between platforms one and two next to Mehmet, the Coffee Guy. We're preparing for the first train of the day, the 5.37. He's going to make the coffee. I'm going to ask the people who buy it how they're feeling. Sevenoaks is Home Counties commuter belt. Most people who live here work in London. They commute five days a week, up and down, up and down. I've done it for the last ten years and I know every single tree, house, back garden, shop, bridge, washing line and discarded beer can from here to London Bridge. But that's nothing. Some of these guys have been doing it for forty years. They can tell you how much journey is left from the shadows playing across their exhausted eyelids as they drift in and out of their un-relenting reality. Sometimes, you see their lips move in time with the announcements. Ashford. Wye. Chilham. Chart-ham. Canterbury West, Minster and Ramsgate. Passengers in the front four carriages for Folkestone West, Folkestone Central, Dover Priory, Mordor. Sometimes their lips stop moving and curl into a semi-conscious smile. It is almost over. In their battered briefcase, you can make out the unmistakable shape of a carriage clock and a Littlewoods voucher. The next day, someone else in pinstripes has taken their seat.

I go in after the stockbrokers and hedge fund managers with the tail end of accountants and lawyers, the bulk of bulk sales managers and the first hysterical flutter of yummy mummies. All these people are, on the whole, fine to share a train with. There is a sense of communal pain. We're in this together, enduring the daily grind, the sheer monotony and occasional horror of getting from A to B on public transport.

It's not all plain sailing. I have minor issues with some of them. The men, for example, who sit in the aisle seat and then spend ages huffily putting their tray up and moving out of the way to let you have the window seat when, frankly, life would have been so much easier if they'd taken the window seat in the first place. And the men, sometimes the same men, who sit like they've got testicles the size of bowling balls, legs apart, knee right over onto my side. No one has testicles that big. And the women who type very loudly as if to say, 'I type loudly because I have very important things to do and very little time in which to do them, as exemplified by the way I am beating my laptop to death with my fake fingernails. Look how I fly through my extensive To Do list while you just sit there getting irritated by something as inconsequential as the sound of my typing. You are such a loser.'

All this is surmountable compared to another group of people, the people who don't fit in, who aren't on the team, who are the Angriest People on Trains. Old People.

Old people on trains are very different from the old people on buses. I can't offer a scientific explanation but they're meaner, tougher, bonier. I would guess that it has something to do with pensions. The old people on buses have retired. Everything has gone quite well. They aren't even having to pay for their bus passes. They are just riding around on the bus, looking out of the window, wondering if it's Tuesday or Wednesday because Tuesday is jam roly-poly day and Wednesday is fish fingers. And that's how I want to be when I'm old.

THINGS HAVEN'T GONE SO WELL for the old people on trains. They are still working. At work, they are surrounded by twenty-five-year-olds with an air of unearned self-importance. Their boss values enthusiasm over experience. These old people are angry and resentful. Of course there are exceptions to this rule. Some old people on trains are quite happy. They're off to a matinee or the bingo or lunch with their Championship goalkeeper son (see Chapter Nine). But on my morning train, they are still going to work and they are just totally pissed off about it.

This manifests itself in different ways. For example, there is Old Person A who always gets the 8.47. You would recognise her because she keeps her head tightly wrapped in a scarf to prevent it from exploding. She has a scowl so intense it could melt the nylon face off a child's favourite soft toy. She stands where she thinks the doors of the train will stop. As the train pulls in, she turns to granite, preventing anyone from bustling her along as they walk with the doors. This is outrageous. Walking with the doors is the fundamental right of every English commuter. If we had a constitution, it would be its third amendment (after 'Every person shall have the right to find Julia Bradbury annoying' and 'Every person shall slack off a bit on Bank Holiday Friday'). If the train goes a little further up the platform than where she has dug herself in, she turns from granite to the bad guy's chariot in *Ben-Hur* and shreds anyone standing between her and the button on the door.

She is not as bad as Old Person B, mainly because she doesn't tell you to fuck off to your face. 'Fuck off!' yells Old Person B at me every time I cycle past her on the way to catch the 8.34, which is really quite breathtaking for someone who could be a granny. Frequently, this is the first bit of conversation I have in the day. She then sits behind me muttering darkly. I once saw her squash a wasp's head between her thumb and her index finger and flick the abdomen down a drain. I once saw her put her foot out on purpose when the man with the drinks trolley came through.

On the whole, though, I have quite a nice commute. And I don't have to be on platform one of Sevenoaks station at half-five in the morning. There are no old people here now. They are all still at home, throwing stones at cats and making a third cup of tea with the same teabag.

In the olden days, the only people catching trains this early would have been the crazy people and the gym freaks.

Now, it's the guys getting up for the foreign markets. The Hang Seng. The Nikkei. The Shenzhen. They've got to be at their desks at half-six. They make lots and lots of money but they're miserable, right? They must be. It would be simply unbearable if they weren't. That's why I'm here, with Mehmet, serving them coffee. I want to confirm what I already know: all the money in the world can't buy happiness at half-five in the morning. Not if you're English and it's drizzling.

'Morning, Chris,' says Mehmet to the first guy to come down the stairs.

'Morning,' replies the fifty-something man. 'The usual, please.'

'Could you tell me how you're feeling right now?' I say brightly. 'Give me a mark out of ten.'

I'm expecting to be dismissed with a shrug or an unnecessary hand gesture or an attempted strangulation. Commuters don't like being asked stuff. I am breaking all sorts of sacred conventions.* But he looks at me and smiles. 'Nine.'

'What?'

---

* The principal one, of course, being that you don't talk to each other unless the train has broken down or is on fire or been sucked up into a flying saucer and transported to a different galaxy for a series of awkward rectal experiments. Then you may talk to each other, but only about the crisis in hand, for example where the aliens are going to put that probe and why, nothing else, except maybe sport or how something similar happened to you on the 6.43 last Thursday.

'Nine.'

'At five thirty-two in the morning? Have you not noticed that it is drizzling?'

'Yes, but it's so peaceful at this time of day.'

The next guy is smiling before he even reaches us. 'Nine.'

'Why?'

'This guy right here. Best coffee in the world.'

A woman is listening in the queue behind him. 'He's wrong,' she says once he's gone off with his latte. 'Six out of ten, maximum.'

Mehmet tells me it's the women who are the trouble-makers. The men just take their coffee and go. If there's ever a problem, it's women. Later, we will discuss whether this means men are more easily broken by the commuter life or whether women are just ruder. But for now, the queue is growing.

'Five, possibly six,' says the next man. 'If it was a Friday, it would be a nine. But it isn't. It's a Monday.'

This is a little bit more like it.

Another woman: seven.

Another man: seven. It would be eight but he did his back in at the weekend.

Another man: 'A cheeky seven. You've got to start the week positive but I'm aware it could spiral at any moment.'

The 5.37 pulls in. I hand the last smiling man his change (I'm doing the money which is incredibly exciting but I don't get a uniform which is not). Off he skips with the nines, the eights, the five and the only-slightly-grumpy six like he's in a *Mary Poppins* remake. I'm amazed. I've always wondered how such an advanced civilisation could have engineered antisocial working hours. It is the American Way. But the 5.37ers don't seem to mind. Nor do the 5.49ers. An eight point five. An eight. Another eight. A minus ten. Only kidding, he says as I make a note. Eight. The average is 7.78 and it isn't even six in the morning.

And then a man – mid-forties, thinning on top, fattening around the midriff, works on the Foreign Exchange – spoils it all. 'Five,' he says after briefly considering taking a swing at me for having the impertinence to ask. 'Same shit, different day. Same damned shit. I'm hung over and it's Monday morning and I've got nothing to look forward to until Friday.'

'It's bad to live for the weekend.'

'I know, but the motivation's gone. There's no real reward. Loads of people earn more than us city boys now. Doctors, lawyers. And we take all the flak while a few bastards on top make all the money. Cheers.'

The cheers is for the coffee Mehmet just handed him. He gets on the 6.03 with an eight, another eight, another eight and a nine. A middle-aged Asian man with a smile so bright it's unnerving in the gloom of the crack of dawn is the first to go for an outright ten even though he just missed the train.

'But you just missed the train and it's drizzling.'

'It's Monday morning. You have to start with the maximum. Otherwise it's WTF. You understand?'

The ancient philosophy of What the Fuck. 'Each Monday, you start with ten and you have the rest of the week to use that ten sparingly. By Friday, you might be down to three or four but it's the weekend. You recharge. Then it's Monday again. Ten.'

The man behind him is also a ten. The WTF philosophy is contagious. The next man is a nine, maybe ten, but I disqualify him because he's going to the south of France tomorrow to play golf which is hateable on every level. Eight, eight and then another woman spoils the 6.14 train contingent with a five.

'It would have been an eight if I hadn't checked my emails.'

'It's ten past six and you already have bad emails?'

'They were sent last night.'

'On a Sunday night? Bad work emails?'

'Yes.' She isn't crying but she definitely blinks back a tear. Or maybe not a tear. The tear equivalent of drizzle. The woman behind her steps forward with a smile and a nine. 'I haven't checked my emails yet,' she says.

For the first hour of a drizzling Monday morning, the average score out of ten for commuter happiness is 8.36. Even accounting for Mehmet's argument – that anyone queuing for his amazing coffee is bound to be happier than anyone who isn't – that's still much, much higher than you would hope. If stockbrokers are this happy at six in the morning, then they must be really, really happy by midday and positively ecstatic by gin o'clock. Which is upsetting.

MAYBE STOCKBROKERS ARE morning people. Maybe trains are so good – so efficient, so clean, so punctual, so well-stocked with fine snacks and beverages – these days that the commute has become the best part of the day. Maybe they really are sorry for the delay to this service and maybe it really was caused by a delay to an earlier service. Maybe we should celebrate the train rather than complain about it. No, come on. There's no need for that language. Let us make some comparisons.

On the Great Northern Railway third-class lunch menu in 1898, guests began with printanier, a light vegetable stew, followed by roast sirloin followed by bread and butter pudding. It cost ten pence or about £9.50 in today's money. Today, in second class on the East Coast Main Line, you can have a microwaved sandwich for only £3 (or four pence in old money). And a selection of Walkers crisps and snacks from just £1.

In the standard British Rail carriages of the 1950s, passengers had to endure big old padded seats with far too much legroom and luggage storage. There were just forty-eight seats per Mark 1 carriage and toilets you had to lock and unlock using an actual lock. How primitive. Now, on the very latest Southeastern trains, they've managed to squeeze in upwards of sixty-four seats per carriage which is lovely and cosy, particularly in the summer. And you get to push a button to lock the loo. A computer then decides whether or not you will be permitted to do all your wee in privacy or whether you get to share half of it with everyone standing outside. You push another button and the computer decides if you can leave. It's very futuristic.

On Southwestern, they're doing even better. Their latest Class 450 Desiro trains (*desiro* meaning 'bloody awful' in Portuguese) offer a seat width of just 16.9 inches. This means they are too narrow for 59 per cent of their passengers 'when you take into account elbows'. This encourages standing which, as we have established in Chapter One, is far healthier than sitting.

Also, travel times have plummeted. Thirty-five years ago, it took thirty-five minutes to get from Sevenoaks to London Charing Cross. Now, it takes just thirty-four minutes, weather/leaves/delays to an earlier service permitting.

Thirty-four minutes is a good commute. Not so short you can't have a G&T and read half a thoroughly absorbing chapter about trains in a thoroughly entertaining book about the English, not so long that you have time to question the point of your existence. It's still a little too long, according to the influential Venetian physicist Cesare Marchetti. In 1994 he wrote a seminal work on the anthropology of human transport in which he argued that we have always adjusted our living conditions to give an average commute of an hour a day. In Neolithic times, when walking was the only means of transport, cavemen stockbrokers wouldn't live more than 2.5 kilometres from the rubble exchange. In medieval times, they could move a little further from the turnip exchange thanks to the horse and cart. As faster modes of transport have been invented, the range has increased, suburbs and commuter towns have developed, we have sprawled both geographically and midriffily. But according to Marchetti's Constant, we still like to keep to the golden half-hour. 'Transportation is the unifying principle of the world,' he wrote.

This works very neatly until you get to the here and now and England and house prices. The Office for National Statistics records that three out of four British commuters still conform to Marchetti's Constant. Bully for them. But the figures are starkly different if you work in London. More than half of London workers now have a commute of more than thirty minutes. One in six travel for more than an hour. Don't be too quick to shed a tear for this growing band of ultra-commuters. They earn more. According to the Office for National Statistics, the time it takes for someone to get to work in the capital is directly proportional to the amount they earn. Which ruins Marchetti's Constant but explains all the happy pinstripes at the crack of dawn in Sevenoaks. It doesn't explain Phil Olson though.

FIVE BLOODY TWENTY-FIVE AGAIN. Another dark, foggy, bleak, drizzly, soul-destroying, godforsaken puddle of a morning. Wednesday, not Monday. That's the main difference. That and the longitude. I am standing outside a house in the middle of the Midlands waiting for Phil. He doesn't have to be at his desk at half-seven in the morning like the hedge funders. He doesn't start until half-nine but there's a problem: his desk is near Heathrow. Phil, a thirty-nine-year-old IT consultant, lives on the outskirts of Sutton Coldfield, which is on the outskirts of Birmingham which is almost four and a half hours from Heathrow. Which means he commutes nine hours a day, five days a week. Which means we're leaving now.

'Morning,' he says, bleary-eyed.

'Morning,' I reply. I had been expecting someone clearly deranged, but, on first impressions, he seems normal. We get into his Citroën C3 and, once the windows have defogged, set off into the still-very-much-night to a car park on the fringes of Birmingham International Airport. From there we canter to the railway station, not the airport ('By the time we've checked in, it would take longer to fly') and stand in a queue for a ticket on the 6.05 a.m. London Midland train. The train will arrive at Euston just after eight, having stopped at Berkswell, Tile Hill, Canley, Coventry, Rugby, Long Buckby, Northampton, Wolverton, Milton Keynes and Leighton Buzzard.

The man in front of us is having a typically Kafkaesque conversation with the woman at the desk as they both attempt to navigate their way through the infinite complexities of the ticketing system.

'It's cheaper if you buy two tickets, one from here to Coventry and one from Coventry to Euston,' says the woman with a shrug.

'Even though I'll be on the same train?' says the man, quite reasonably.

'Yes.'

'Fine.'

'It just works out that way.'

Some time later, we set off on stage two of the epic commute. 'At this point, I'll normally put my headphones on,' says Phil, clearly wishing that he hadn't agreed to let me join him. 'I have a relaxation tape on my phone, a thunder-and-rain storm which blocks out all the noise of the announcements. I can catch up on sleep until Milton Keynes. That's when it fills up. I've had someone pull out my earphones and ask me to budge up before.'

Six-fifteen and we've got as far as Berkswell. I ask Phil if, given the correlation between long commutes and large salaries, he earns a bomb.

'Sadly not,' he says, as we watch nine other suits clamber on at Rugby. 'The extra money I get working in London pays for the extra travel costs, and it's a great job for the CV, but I'm not rolling in it.'

This is why we're stuck on the 6.05 a.m. train. There is an express train leaving five minutes earlier that is almost twice as fast and stops hardly anywhere, but Phil says it would cost him £6,000 more a year. Britain's high-speed intercity trains might be making long-distance commutes relatively painless, they might even be aspiring to Marchetti's Constant,* but you pay a premium to go fast. These days, the defining class systems on routes to and from London, Birmingham, Manchester and beyond are no longer first and second, they're Quick and Very Slow. For example, if you want to live in the delightful environs of York and work in the less delightful environs of London, it will cost an eye-watering £12,300 a year to commute on the high-speed East Coast line (not including the microwaved sandwich).

Or you can screw Marchetti and take the slow train. Like Phil. But this has consequences. Researchers at Umea University in Sweden, a country blessed with an excellent, stress-free public transport infrastructure, found that couples in which one partner commutes for longer than forty-five minutes are 40 per cent more likely to get divorced. Other researchers have found disproportionate levels of pain, obesity and stress in long-distance commuters. All those years listening to half a mobile phone conversation, sweating away in an overcrowded carriage, sniffing the armpit of the moist quantity surveyor in front of you . . . It can't be healthy.

Robert Putnam, the Harvard political scientist, suggests that long commuting times are directly linked to social

* He envisaged the potential for cities of a billion people if the average speed of the commute was above 140km/h. A sort of Maglev-meets-*Blade Runner* future. Fat chance.

isolation. For every ten minutes longer on the train, your life has 10 per cent fewer social connections. For every ten minutes, you are more likely to miss dinner or the start of the school nativity. Or celebrate your wedding anniversary by text.

Eight o'clock and a bit. Contrary to the findings of Harvard scientists, Phil and I have managed to connect socially on our epic journey into Euston. And in spite of the Swedish doom and the Harvard gloom, Phil doesn't seem 40 per cent more likely to divorce either. He met his future wife after calling to report a faulty mobile phone. He chatted to the girl at the call centre for more than an hour. By the end, he had Lisa's phone number. They met that weekend and never looked back. He got a wife. She got the sack. It is the most romantic story I've ever heard from a man called Phil.

We still aren't anywhere near his office though. We're trudging across to Euston Square to catch the Circle Line Tube. Then we stand all the way to Edgware Road before walking to a bus stop where Phil must wait ten minutes for a work coach to take him out to an office park just off the A4. He's going to wait alone. I'm off to buy triple espresso, a Red Bull, a Monster Java, three Mars Bars, an Egg McMuffin and another triple espresso.

'I'll get to my desk at half-nine and everyone will look at me like I'm mad,' he says like he's mad as we say our good-byes. 'I couldn't do this for ever.'

A lot of commuters say that – but I believe him. Nobody can do nine hours a day for very long, can they? Can they? Can they, Phil? That night, I'm asleep by eight, just as Phil is passing back through Milton Keynes. And I suspect he will have a contented smile on his face. The day is almost done. He is on his way back home, back to Lisa. It's almost meditative.

THERE IS A REASON why there are many poems about trains and virtually none about motorways (no, Chris Rea does not count). It's the same reason Celia Johnson has her brief encounter with Trevor Howard at a railway station rather than a National Express depot. And why it's *Murder on the Orient Express*, not *Slight Bludgeoning on the Rail Replacement Service to Orpington*. The reason is romance.

Get on a train anywhere in England, absolutely anywhere. Yes, even Swindon. Sit by the window. Yes, I'm making an assumption that there is a window seat available. Put away your phone, your other phone, your iPod, your iPad, your laptop, your e-reader . . . oh God, are you on it now? Are you reading this on a Kindle? That is so Buck Rogers/*Fahrenheit 451*. Well, keep going – you are the future. Everyone else, put all your gizmos away and look out of the window. Isn't it beautiful, all that stuff out there, rushing by? (And yes, all right, again I'm making assumptions that your train is capable of rushing and that it's not pitch black and you're not called Phil and all you can see is your own mad, haggard reflection staring back at you.) It's beautiful, right?

Right?

I'm on one of those Pendolinos to Birmingham New Street and this isn't, by several hours, a commuter train (there are only four people in my carriage and my ticket didn't cost £456,143). It's a fresh late autumn afternoon and England is racing by in a satisfying 125mph blur. There's a churchyard, a housing estate, twenty green fields in a row, a scrap metal dealership, a gasworks, a traffic jam. Haha-haha, a traffic jam. You lose, traffic. I win.

Horses . . . more horses . . . more bloody horses. We still have a lot of horses in this day and age, don't we? Office parks, car parks, industrial parks, caravan parks full of cara-vans full of people who must think it's absolutely brilliant to (a) have a caravan and (b) park it right next to a high-speed rail line. There's an out-of-town carpet centre with, hang on, no, it can't be, stop the train, pull the emergency cord . . . the carpet centre has a sale on. It's offering, wow, I can hardly believe it, up to 60 per cent off ABSOLUTELY EVERYTHING. One week only. Stop the— oh, bum. It's gone. If only I'd been in that traffic jam.

A secondary school with children being forced to play rugby and an enormous canvas banner advertising its web-site like it's an out-of-town carpet centre. Ponds, lakes, rivers, reservoirs all trying to cope with the last seven days' deluge. A large company called Euro-bearings Ltd which either sells ball-bearings to the French or sells strong perspectives about the French to everyone else.* A spire in the middle distance, the tallest building for as far as the eye can see, just as it has been for the previous half millennium and counting, more constant than anything Marchetti could come up with. Then gone in a flash.

An Englishman's urge to complain about commuting might pass the time but it is superficial. Beneath it, there is a love affair, not a smouldering Spanish one with tongues and torn T-shirts, but something a little more discreet and easily neglected.

I will not neglect you any more, I decided right there at Birmingham New Street. I'm not ready to become a train-spotter, *mon chéri*, but I will be more positive. I will love my commute. I will follow the WTF philosophy. I will enjoy the blur of humanity outside the English train window because it is better than the blur of kangaroo outside the Indian Pacific train window from Perth to Sydney, and everyone raves about that.**

---

* Didn't want this bugging you so I looked them up. The company was started in 1983 by Sue and Gerry Smith. Primarily 'the product range manufactured is for truck mast bearings and these are distributed to end users, bearing distributors and original equipment manufacturers in the UK and to these types of customers in other countries.' They also do combined roller bearings, anti-vibration mountings, mating steel profiles, ball transfer units and shaft-mounted linear bearings. Who knew bearings could be so sexy?

** I have been one of those ravers because it's an epic rail journey. Can't recommend it enough if you happen to be in Perth and you're trying to get to Sydney and you're terrified of flying. The view can get a bit, well, samey, on those 4,352 kilometres compared to England's comparatively infinite variety. Still, grass is always greener . . .

MY RESOLUTION LASTS THREE DAYS and then I dare to go to the pub after work and have one for the road and another for the road and, even though at my age I worry about the hangover even before I start drinking, another for the road. Consequently I miss the last fast train and have to get the Absolute Last Absolutely Not Fast Train which stops everywhere and is known locally as the Vomit Comet, not because it is part of the NASA Reduced Gravity Research Program [sic] but because people tend to throw up on it [sick], and tonight, as the world doesn't fly by, but chugs by, people called Lance and Chardonnay become embroiled in drunken rows and everyone else is expected to pretend they can't hear.

'I can't believe you think I slept with Tracy. Why would I have sex with her?'

'Maybe because she's a slut?'

'She's a minger.'

'Oh, so that's the only thing stopping you, is it?'

'She's a right pain in the arse.'

'Well, you spent all night talking to her, didn't ya?'

'She was talking to me, wasn't she? What am I supposed to do?'

'Tell her you're with me.'

'She knows I'm with you.'

'Piss off, Lance.'

'You piss off, Chardonnay.'

'I love you though, don't I?'

'You do though, don't you?'

'I do though, don't I?'

'Ahhh, you're so romantic. Isn't he romantic?'

'Umm, yes, madam. He is jolly romantic.'

'Are you taking the piss, mate?'

'Yeah, are you taking the piss?' *(Estás a gozar ?)*

'*Bing bong. The next station will be Sevenoaks. Please remember to take all your personal belongings with you before you get off the train. Not after. Because that will be too late.*'

I would have asked Lance and Chardonnay how they were feeling out of ten, but (a) you ask them and (b) they would only have said 8.5. People on trains are, weirdly, happy. Happy because they are miserable, maybe, but happy all the same. As Lance and Chardonnay, the two young lovers, demonstrate, we haven't moved too far from *Brief Encounter*. The train, despite all the complaining, despite where it is taking us or what it is taking us from, is still one of the most romantic parts of English life. Even when it's late. Even when it's taking us to work.

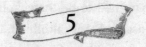

THE OFFICE

*I don't live by 'The Rules' you know, and if there's one
person who has influenced me in that way of thinking,
someone who is a maverick, someone who does 'that' to
the system then it's Ian Botham.*

DAVID BRENT, visionary boss

THE OFFICE. NINE TO FIVE. Eight to six. Worse? I'm
sorry. The thin, noncommittal smiles in the lift. Morning.
Morning. I hate you. I hate you too. The computer that
decides, no, insists you need to update your password and
the knowledge that it is right to insist because otherwise
your password would still be the city where you met your
third girlfriend many decades ago. The boss with his/her
whiteboard, his/her sofa and his/her false charm offensives
and power trips and insecurities. The colleagues with their
pink Post-it notes and their habits. Chair-rocking. Pacing.
Sighing. Tutting. Humming. Complaining. Eating crisps.
Complaining. Watching virals. Complaining. Holding the

computer responsible for their own inadequacies. And the other side effects of our open-plan culture. The loud phone conversations about her wedding, his medical condition, their hilarious, you-had-to-be-there holiday capers. The healthy food consumed unhealthily at the desk. Salads. Hummus sandwiches. Moccafrappaskinnysoyalattes. I'm just getting a tea. Do you want one? Thought not. The plastic monkey that does a somersault when you wind it up. The gradual realisation that the plastic monkey is you.

We must put these trivialities aside and celebrate all that is wonderful about the office. Such as . . .

Umm.

Errr.

Hang on a minute . . . nope. It's gone.

No, wait . . .

Yes, right. The office romance, that most unlikely of concepts because romance should be the last thing on our minds but it isn't. Seventy per cent of us have found love and kisses amid the spreadsheets and PowerPoints. The office, as opposed to the bar, the nightclub and the internet dating website, is the place to find the One. Laura is Welsh but has agreed* to be English for the purposes of this chapter, and in order to tell her 'sordid tale of debauchery' set in the London offices of a private medical insurance company.

It is late in 2007 and Laura, thirty-one, is busy in the 'sexy' training and development department of her Fins-

---

* Very, very reluctantly.

bury Square employer. She is already seeing a colleague from Australia. He is 'a bit of a knob'.

Tom, thirty-two, who looks and sounds like Hugh Grant but is actually from Wiltshire,* is Head of Compliance and Risk. He sits in a separate section from the rest of the office 'because of the sensitive nature of his work', he says (although everyone else says it's because no one wants to sit near anything to do with compliance). He is seeing a girl in marketing.

Tom and Laura have not yet met.

'Hi, we haven't met,' says Tom to Laura. 'I'm Tom, Head of Compliance and Risk and I've heard you've written an excellent training manual. Please could you send me a copy?'

Tom would later admit he never read the report. No interest whatsoever. It was a move, one of the most improbable moves in the history of romance, but with the benefit of hindsight, it worked. 'He had me at head of compliance,' says Laura.

Without the benefit of hindsight, things were a little more complicated than that. Even before they have properly met, the odds are stacked against Laura and Tom. First of all, Laura had just agreed to relocate to Sydney with the 'bit of a knob'. She had already resigned. Once the training

---

* In his first proper conversation with Laura, he would claim he was from Bath but this would be a lie. He is from Corsham. He can't remember when his accent changed from the Wurzels to something more received but it may have been at university.

manual was written, she was gone. Sydney is 10,600 miles from the compliance department. Too far, even for Tom and his hypnotic chat-up lines. Second, the marketing girl was hardly going to walk away from her Hugh Grant without a fight. Third, it might just not happen. Love, as I'm sure you know, can be a fickle thing.

But then comes the Christmas office party which, if Christmas office party surveys are to be believed, improves the prospects of a Tom–Laura hook-up no end. In a *GMTV* survey, 16.4 per cent of office workers claimed they had become intimate with a colleague at their Christmas party. A third of respondents in a survey conducted by a condom manufacturer said they had had sex with a fellow employee during (!) or after their office party. A survey of Londoners not conducted by a condom manufacturer found that one in ten respondents started a relationship at the company Christmas party. A quarter of those questioned said that's how they met their future spouse. A survey of men's mag readers found almost half of respondents had started an affair at a Christmas works' drinks.

Excluding the ridiculous men's mag result and taking an average of the rest, the answer still appears to be that an awful lot of people use the office party as an opportunity to throw themselves at colleagues. And those colleagues appear to be quite receptive to the idea.

What if you don't believe the surveys? This much office-related romance does seem improbable. Four Septembers ago, I got incontrovertible proof. There I was, holding Wife's hand as she gave birth to our second son in a hospital in Kent. An hour later, I was mopping her brow on the post-natal ward which was noticeably packed. Not quite Florence Nightingale doing triage in the corridors but certainly a lot of pale and exhausted first-time mums staring astonished at their brand-new bundles of joy.

'It's very busy,' I pointed out helpfully to the fraught midwife.

'Third week of September,' she pointed out back.

'What does that mean?'

'Forty weeks after the Christmas party.'

'Really?'

'Really.' And she winked. Possibly a just-kidding wink. Possibly not.

I looked around the ward a little more judgementally. Nine months earlier, how many of these women had been dancing on tables to George Michael's 'Last Christmas' while scheming Heads of Compliance ordered yet another round of flaming sambucas?

At Laura's Christmas party, this being a relatively classy story, Tom isn't ordering flaming sambucas. He is trying to avoid the marketing girl, who he has, rather un-festively, dumped. The marketing girl is upset. Laura is comforting the upset marketing girl which will turn out to be karmically ironic. Some other people are snogging. Some different other people are crying. One person is finally, furiously, cathartically telling another person how much she absolutely bloody well hates the way he types so exaggeratedly. But as far as Tom, Laura and their as yet unconceived children are concerned, nothing.

Nothing except a conversation, a conversation that ends with Tom calling Laura a slag as a joke. The next morning, he emails to apologise and says it was nice to chat. And although Laura is attracted to Tom, it was not the sort of attraction that makes you tear up a transglobal plane ticket.

The End.

Or it would have been if Tom's magic compliance powers hadn't begun to take effect. Christmas arrives and Laura is home at her parents. She begins to have second thoughts about emigrating to Sydney. The Australian is 'a bit of a knob', after all. You don't fly 10,600 miles for 'a bit of a knob', do you?

As the New Year arrives, Laura's back goes. Nothing to do with Tom. His magic powers are not that evil. It is a slipped disc. Instead of flying to Sydney, our English-ish heroine finds herself in hospital having an operation. Tom visits which 'at the time I thought was very odd,' recalls Laura. But Tom is a Love Jedi. He knows when to use his love sabre.* The very minute she can walk again, he makes his move. Cue slushy music, a volley of Cupid's arrows and weeks of secret leg-fondling under tables at office pub quiz nights (the only thing worse than office Christmas parties).

* Metaphorically speaking.

'Within a month I had moved into his flat in Tooting Bec and then we got unexpectedly pregnant.' Today, Tom tells people he regarded Laura as a flight risk, what with the 'bit of a knob' waiting in Sydney. Knocking her up was the only option. Slightly evil magic powers after all.

Two years later, pregnant again, Laura marries Tom at the Little White Wedding Chapel in Vegas – a double-barrel shotgun wedding. 'Classy,' says Laura. I told you.

'Do you recommend office romances though?' I ask her.

'I totally recommend them,' she says. 'We meet some of our lifelong friends in the workplace so why not our life partner? Not sure I would have an office random shag though. I think that's when it gets awkward.'

WHEN PEOPLE AREN'T FALLING IN LOVE, what happens in the office? Are we more like the French, God forbid, or the Americans, God forbid? We need a randomly selected French office worker and a randomly selected American and then we can decide. Welcome Marcel, a forty-something chargé d'affaires in a large design company just outside Paris and Erica, a thirty-something assistant director at a merchandising company in Manhattan.

It is nine o'clock on Monday morning and Erica has just started work. Marcel has been going for an hour already but don't feel too sorry for him. You'll probably hate him by the end of the day.

Because he is graded as a senior manager, Marcel has a nice desk by an openable window a long way from *les toilettes*. In France, the grade is everything. It determines your place in the pecking order which in turn determines everything from desk size to aeroplane seat pitch. This isn't particularly surprising. The fatter the cat, the more milk it gets whatever its nationality. But for Marcel, it goes further. It determines who will help him and who won't. If a colleague outgrades him, regardless of any personal friendship, he will have his work cut out getting cooperation. It will also mean he must '*vous-voi*' them rather than '*tu-toi*' them and shake hands with them rather than kiss them. Formality and structure is *très important en France*. Or as Marcel puts it before he takes a break for coffee, 'Hierarchy is very close to our hearts. We celebrate it whereas you are quite embarrassed about it in England, *non*?'

'I don't care at all about my title,' says Erica, who sits in a beige cubicle with beige walls high enough to block out the view of colleagues but not high enough to make it feel as if she has her own private office. 'I only cared when I became an assistant director because my pay went up $10,000. People who really care about job titles are insecure. They think a title proves something about their abilities because their actual ability doesn't.'

Erica does not respect her boss. She wouldn't *vous-voi* her, she'd try not to *tu-toi* her and she would kiss her over her dead body. 'My boss has a horrible temper and never listens and ends up asking ridiculous questions because she has not been listening,' Erica explains, exasperated. 'About 25 per cent of my job is anticipating her misinterpretations, overreactions or mood swings, and explaining to her in soothing tones what is going on, why it is going on, and what we're going to do about it.'

Erica likes her 'co-workers' but they can be, as she puts it, super-annoying.* 'For example, the guy who sits across the aisle from me spends hours every day talking about baseball. I had no idea there was so much to say about baseball but, apparently, there is. HOURS. EVERY DAY.'

This morning, the woman across the other aisle has made two phone calls to order a horse for her fiancé to ride in on at her wedding. Groom-on-horse woman and baseball guy have also had very loud half-hour hysterics about another colleague who had to share a bed with his boss when their hotel was overbooked. 'I mean, sure, giggle about it once,' says Erica. 'But making jokes for a half-hour? Are they twelve?'

Back across the Atlantic, it is not done to talk loudly in Marcel's office (which, by the way, also does a fine line in beige and is quite minimalist – the personalising of desks with executive stress toys, novelty staplers, plastic monkeys that do somersaults and the like are frowned upon). 'You talk in the conviviality area,' he explains.

---

* American for very annoying.

The conviviality area?

'It is very convivial. There are coffee machines and comfy chairs, a shoe polishing machine and two big television screens, one with a news channel and one with *Eurosport*.'

Parfait.

Like, whatever.

MIDDAY AND MARCEL is off for lunch and if you're the sort of person who lives somewhere leafy and entrenched and you find the teachings of UKIP most enriching, look away now. French companies have to pay for their employees' lunch, or contribute to most of it. Marcel used to eat out every day with all his colleagues – set menus are available in every bar and restaurant in the country. Now his company has a canteen but you must banish that picture of a work canteen that just sprang into your mind. Marcel's canteen has a salad bar, a grill serving all manner of fine meats from steak to black pudding, as well as menus with two fish dishes, a meat dish, vegetables, fruit and cheeses. There is a dessert bar and a drinks counter with, *naturellement*, soft drinks, wine and beer. And it's all subsidised: three courses for less than £3. Today, Marcel has the bouillabaisse. If the weather had been better, he might have gone out to the local open-air swimming pool before taking lunch at a café. He has two hours, after all, and he will always start prompt at midday.

'We are very punctual,' he explains. 'I could not be late for my afternoon appointment so if I started lunch late I would have to rush it. Of course, this would be unforgivable.'

Sometimes, if there are no afternoon appointments, lunch can run over. His record is twelve hours.

Erica is allowed forty-five minutes for her lunch but usually manages just half an hour at her desk. On most days, she gets a salad to go from the deli nine floors down and one street across. Her $9 salad has a lettuce base to which she can add five further ingredients. Today, she picks carrots, tomatoes, broccoli, chickpeas and grape leaves. As if that isn't bad enough, she goes for the fat-free ranch dressing which is, inevitably, a mistake.

'Occasionally my boss will bring our team out for lunch and that is always somewhere expensive,' she says. 'We spend hours eating and that's all well and good except that nobody likes my boss and we would all rather just eat a cheap lunch by ourselves.'

The afternoon has arrived. Marcel is feeling very relaxed and happy after his long lunch. Erica is not. She has back-to-back meetings and for her, meetings mean PowerPoint. 'People love PowerPoints. They really love them. Usually these PowerPoints are explaining things that could be explained much more efficiently with no PowerPoint.' This is as much an English disease as an American one – death by bullet point. Nasty. 'Also,' she continues, 'people love proposing ideas and arguing about ideas but nobody loves coming to a conclusion. I don't think I've ever been in a meeting where anything is actually decided.'

Marcel? 'We can talk a lot and everyone wants to have the last word so without a *force majeure*, meetings can go on indefinitely,' he admits. 'If you want to keep it short, it's usually better to schedule it before lunch. That way, it will never overrun.'

At five in the afternoon, Erica is out of there. By working through lunch, she can knock off early. Every now and again, she might feel the pressure to attend one of the company's social evenings which have 'horribly embarrassing themes such as luau and hipster', but not today. Her friends in other offices also have nine-to-five contracts but she is the only one to get out on time. Work-hour creep is endemic in Manhattan. She also 'lucked out' with twenty days of holiday a year, generous compared to other US offices. There is no statutory minimum but the average is fifteen days a year. Ten is not uncommon. Ten.

Most English people have lucked out even more than Erica. The statutory holiday allowance is now a not-too-shabby twenty-eight days, the highest in Europe. But Marcel and his Gallic chums have super-lucked out. Sure, he will be in the office for an hour longer than Erica tonight. That's an eight-hour day and a forty-hour week. But as of 2000, no Frenchman can work more than an average of thirty-five hours per week over the year. So Marcel gets working time recuperation on top of holiday. Last year, he took two months off. *Formidable*.

It's not a competition. Well, it is. And where you come in it depends entirely on your own office. Are you lucky enough to have a continental approach to the lunch hour? Are your employers all blue-sky American? Is everything beige? Of course it is. In an ideal world, we'd take Marcel's canteen and Erica's five o'clock escape, and maybe her English muffin when she wasn't looking. We're not in an ideal world though. We're in England. The closest you get to ideal, according to its own promotional video, is Cobalt Office Park, North Tyneside.

'HELLO,' says a girl on a bicycle to a girl getting out of her Toyota Prius.

'Morning, pet,' replies the girl, waving her hair around as if Pantene Pro-V really does give the natural volume of which she'd always dreamed.

'Hiya,' says a man beside a bush to a woman getting off a bus.

'Hiya,' replies the woman.

'Morning, love,' says a woman cartwheeling through the revolving doors of her office with no concern for her health or safety.

'Morning,' says the security guard, his straight white teeth glinting in the sun.*

This isn't even the promotional video. This is actually happening in real life. I'm right in the middle of Cobalt and people are all saying hello to each other in a genuine,

* See The Terrifying Rise of Teeth-Whitening Kiosks, Chapter Seven.

happy way even though they're arriving at work, not leaving it. This may be because someone has put something in the water. It may be a cult. Or the sequel to the *Truman Show* – and nobody told me. Or it may simply be that the sun is shining *and* it is warm, two meteorological events that are rare enough on their own up here.* Whatever the reason, it is distinctly unsettling.

Cobalt is the largest office park in Europe. It is a small city of glass, steel, light, air and yellow bricks, 1.7 million feet of office space connected by bendy roads, low-carbon bus lanes and jogging tracks. It looks like an architectural model, perfectly laid out, perfectly planted, calculated for maximum worker efficiency. To a cynical outsider, it could be construed as completely and utterly soulless. There is a theme pub in a theme hotel, the only pub for miles and miles, there are crèche facilities and a 'five-hundred delegate conference facility'. There are hubs and data banks and business suites called 'Energy' and 'Vision', and one coffee shop, a Starbucks, with signs on its terrace saying, 'To protect the quality of our coffee, we ask you not to smoke.' Which is almost enough to make you start smoking. Because it's not their coffee. It's ours. We just bought it.

'Hiya,' says Pam, a potentially cult-inducted employee of a mobile phone company based at Cobalt.

---

* It is frequently sunny and absolutely blimming freezing in the north-east. The last time it was sunny and not absolutely blimming freezing was in August 1649. Fourteen local women were hanged on Newcastle Moor as a result.

'Hiya,' I reply. It's contagious.

'Shall we have a look around?' she says.

'Yes,' I reply, grinning. She walks me around the mega-open-plan airport-hangar-size call centres, each one handling a different aspect of mobile phonery. Press one for customer services and you get through to the endlessly patient teams in hangar one. Press two if you are a new customer and ping, you'll be through to the piranhas, sorry 'incoming sales' teams, in hangar two. Press three if you are thinking of leaving us and you'll get the lilting voices, silver tongues and magic promises of the naughty gigolos in hangar three. Hangar four, debt collection for when that phone the nice lady in hanger two flogged you becomes a bit much. Hangar five, outbound sales. 'The hardcore,' says Pam.

'We believe in giving the UK the best network and best service so that customers trust us with their digital lives,' says a banner slung across a far wall next to a digital scoreboard of call-waiting times. The wait to get through to someone in faults? Two hundred and seventeen seconds. The wait to get through to someone in small-business sales? Six seconds.

'And that's where we have the buzz sessions,' says Pam.

'The what?'

'The buzz sessions.'

'The what?'

'The buzz sessions. It's a ten-minute pep talk each morning with the team manager. And that's the water cooler which is where we normally go after the buzz session to complain about the team manager. Hahaha.'

'Hahahaha.'

'Wouldn't you rather work in an office in Newcastle? Right in the centre? Next to shops and cafés and art galleries and . . . life.'

'No, it's great here,' says Pam. 'It's a much quicker journey too.'

Pam glides off on invisible rollerblades, perhaps the happiest person I have ever met. There is no cult. She is not brainwashed. She actually likes her office park. And so does Lyn who works for Cobalt itself.

'There's not much here besides offices though,' I suggest pityingly.

'Well, I think what Cobalt is doing now is that it's developing a business community. We're building on that. Cobalt did not want to build a load of buildings with no sense of being together. So that's why we've launched More Cobalt which has activities and events and discounts and there's a Facebook grou—'

'It's a bit corporate, isn't it?' I interrupt, because it's all getting a bit corporate. 'I bet no one real is on a Cobalt Facebook page.'

'It is real, I promise. Just have a look. And we just ran the moron show event which took over the empty building next door.'

'I'm sorry?'

'The moron show.'

'What's a moron show?'

'No, sorry. More. Separate word. On. Show. More On Show.'

'Wow.'

'Sorry, it must have been my way of pronouncing it. It was an exhibition to showcase all the things going on at Cobalt.'

'Like what?'

'We have a Cobalt netball team, a five-a-side team, a walk group.'

'Where do you go walking? Round all the offices?'

'We have a thirty-nine-acre nature park attached to the business park. It's gorgeous. It's the highest point in Tyneside. You can see all the way to the coast. Out-of-town offices are having to do more to compete with the town centres. You have to offer extra incentives and you have to concentrate on the environment. We have a three-metre floor-to-ceiling height for example which is very high.'

'So workers don't feel like slaves?'

'Umm, yes. And we have lots of green space and wildlife.'

'Like what?'

'Like deer. Roe deer.'

'Really? Here?'

'I haven't seen her for a while though.'

'There's just one?'

'Two. But there are hawks and oyster catchers and . . .'

This is the twenty-first-century factory. The coalmines and steelworks are shut and this is what has replaced them, almost literally. The footpaths that crisscross Cobalt used to be a network of wagon trails for getting coals to Newcastle.

Now they are used by the thousands of service-industry workers stepping out from their own white-collar coalface. It is anonymous, manufactured, deeply, deeply controlled, but it could be a lot worse.

COULD IT BE A LOT BETTER THOUGH? Could offices ever be fun? Actually fun rather than MoreOn fun? They can be if you work in California and you understand programming and you are, like, so still in your twenties. Google's head office, the Googleplex of course, is a particularly nauseating example of how Silicon Valley start-ups are rejecting the cardinal rule that offices must be beige. There are lava lamps and exercise balls and campus bicycles and pool tables. No employee must be more than 100 feet from free food, which is a little bit French but also as far from being French as it is possible to be. Pets are allowed to wander the corridors. There's a replica spaceship in the foyer. If you don't believe me, Google it.

In England, we don't have the Californian climate but we have got our very own Silicon Valley. Sort of. It's called Silicon Roundabout which is immediately less sexy. Also, technically speaking, it is Old Street Roundabout in east London, the most miserable roundabout in the whole capital except for Elephant and Castle, and it isn't made of silicon. It is 40 per cent concrete, 40 per cent tarmac, 20 per cent tramp wee. But this is supposedly the place where the future, the wonderful, depressing, ridiculous, nourishing, unnourishing app-based, cybernetic future is made by people who are implausibly young and live in Shoreditch and spend more money on their headphones than their sustenance. And talk to each other in Javascriptenese.

Do these people exist or are they just a figment of other, old, jealous people's imaginations? As I sit on a multi-coloured, multi-patterned, multi-textured, bias-cut sofa in the reception area of Office 4.01 of the Tea Building, Shoreditch High Street, under a ceiling of plastic ivy in front of a mismatched dining table and chairs and a sign saying, 'Here be monsters' and another sign saying, 'Work hard and be nice to people', as chill-out music wafts over the heads of assorted skinny, pasty, enthusiastic T-shirted 'hipsters' making themselves chociattos in the smoothie-making zone of a company called Mind Candy, I can confirm that they do exist. Very much so.

Mind Candy is the company that came up with Moshi Monsters which, as you will know because you are totally down with the kids, is an online world where children are encouraged to nurture virtual monsters and interact with other children nurturing other virtual monsters. The nurturing is quite straightforward. Play with it! Tickle it! Feed it! If you're serious about it, which you are because you are a child and the last thing you want on your hands is a neglected pet monster, you must plant seeds in your Moshling garden which will attract Moshlings which you keep in a Moshling Zoo. Why? Because the Moshi Monsters like to keep the Moshlings as pets. It's a responsibility double-down. Then there's Dr Strangeglove who few people in this building remember from the first time around. He is the Moshi Monsters' arch-enemy and can only be beaten by the Supermoshis. Then there are the bobblebots . . .

Don't scoff. At the time of writing, 50 million of these virtual pets have been adopted by non-virtual children. Which means 100 million by the time of reading. And a billion by half past four tomorrow. It's a huge hit, an Angry Bird meets Facebook for seven-year-olds. And, inevitably, it is now accompanied by real-life merchandise. (Daddy, pllllleeease can I have Moshi Monsters Moshling Tree-house for only £54.21?) This is why everyone looks so happy in Office 4.01 of the Tea Building. Michael Smith, the entrepreneurial hipster boss and the man who invented the shot-glass chessboard,* is away on a road trip across America with friends because why the hell not. So I have hipster Nicole to show me around. Once she's made her chociatto of course.

'I'm just going to get a chociatto,' she says. 'You're not going to put that in, are you?'

I ask her why everyone looks so happy, so nauseatingly pleased to be at work.

'It's the people, really,' she says. 'It's like a family.'

And that isn't even in the Top Ten Things About Mind Candy That Will Make Anyone Who Doesn't Work at

---

* Not quite worthy of a place in the Hall of Life-Changing Stuff Invented by the English. The shot-glass chess set, sold by Michael Smith's first company Firebox, was no Teasmade but it does force you to improve your game fast.

Mind Candy Want to Scream. Number one, once a month they have a sort of gourmet feast/picnic on beanbags and green carpets so everyone can just, you know, catch up and chill. Number two, one of the employees is called the Chief Moshiologist. Three, on lunchtimes when they aren't having a gourmet picnic, they have a Game Jam which is 'like a little hackathon'.

'What's a little hackathon?' I ask, wishing I'd brought a baseball cap and that I was wearing it the wrong way around and that my name was Sergei and my girlfriend was called Cybertwirl and that we met online while breaking into the Pentagon's mainframe. People peer from behind their Macs to see exactly which dinosaur had never heard of the word hackathon.

'It's when you hack ideas together [you idiot].'

'A brainstorm then?'

'Sort of. [Who is this chump?]'

'A blue-sky meeting?'

'No. [He must be, like, someone from the olden days when apparently they had to dial up their broadband and watch television on an actual television and did something called emailing.]'

The idea of Game Jam is that someone generates a name of a game using either their brain or a computer program they have designed specifically for the purpose. Then, using pipe cleaners, paper, glue, cardboard and/or more programming, they have one hour to make that game.

Four, 'Sometimes, if we're stressed, we pile up beanbags

in a big heap and somersault onto them. You should try it. It will really help you de-stress. Go on, try it. Try it. Why won't you try it?'

Five and six, the treehouse meeting area (because the boss likes treehouses) and the doodlewall (because it's good to doodle). And seven, the fact that dance-chart-topping Hed Kandi played their Christmas staff party while everyone else in the country had to make do with Dave and his Razzle-dazzle Portable Turntables. And eight, they all made each other Hed Kandi head candy* on the night.

Number nine, 'Yeah, we do socialise with each other, don't we, Maz? The other night we were all here until ten.'

'Working?'

'No, it was games club.'

'The hackathon thingy?'

'No, we played Pandemic.'**

'Oh right. An iPad app? Right on.'

'No, the board game. It was old-school. We were playing for hours.'

'Rad.'

And number ten, the tenth and most wonderful thing for Mind Candy employees and the most grating thing for

---

* Face masks. Keep up.

** What do you mean, you haven't heard of Pandemic? You are like so not with it, dude. It's a cooperative board game, obviously. Four diseases have broken out in the world and it is up to a team of specialists in various fields to find cures for these diseases before mankind is wiped out. Totally cool way to spend an evening.

everyone else, the all-round, all-pervasive happiness vibe. Even the marketing manager is happy. Most of us don't skip into work, love every minute of it and then refuse to leave until you've spent at least four hours of an evening jamming or hacking or drinking or all three with your co-workers. Most of us schlep into work, huff around a bit, make wry jokes with your mates on email, hope those jokes don't go viral, and then go home, living for the evening on the sofa and the weekend in the pub.

An ancient poet and philosopher once wrote: 'Workin' Nine to Five, oh what a way to make a livin', barely gettin' by, it's all takin' and no givin'. They just use your mind and they never give you credit.'

This might be coming to an end. Not the last bit but certainly the rest of it. The future might be work-life balance, holistic happiness in the workplace, beanbags, hackathons.

'Don't you ever get grumpy and stressed here?' I ask Nicola as I call the very trendy goods lift to take me back to the present.

'Sometimes things can get a little fraught,' she replies. 'But that's only because we're passionate about what we do. Byeeeeeee.'*

I step back from this horrifying, beautiful, bionic version of the future into the present. It's the end of the week. It's the beginning of the weekend. And I need a drink.

---

* She didn't say 'Byeeeeeee'. She said, 'Bye.' Nobody in Shoreditch says 'Byeeeee'. I'm sorry.

THE PUB, THE CLUB
AND THE BALTI HOUSE

Man being reasonable must get drunk; The best of life is but intoxication; Glory, the grape, love, gold – in these are sunk – The hopes of all men and of every nation.

GEORGE BYRON, party animal

A WOMAN SITS IN THE damp gutter, legs sprawled, head bowed, viscose chemise slipping. Her friend is trying to get her to stand up but between them they have the balance of a newly born alpaca. They collapse back down and start laughing and then someone across the road shouts something deeply derogatory and the camera moves away.

'Across the UK, a culture of weekend binge-drinking is in full swing,' says our grim-jawed guide at the start of Channel 4's *Party Paramedics*. 'In the battle to deal with over a million drink-related casualties each year, there is a new front line.'

The new front line is not really a front line. It's a bus in which some volunteers stitch up and make coffee for drunk, slightly wounded people in Colchester. If anything, it's quite civilised. The volunteers are like your mum when you've scraped your knee on the way home from school, all 'there, there' and 'don't worry, pet' and warm flannels. The drunk revellers are sheepish and grateful. *Party Paramedics* should have been called *Nice Community Project in Which Selfless People Help Out a Small Minority of Young People Who Took Their Partying Too Far*. Less catchy but honestly, if you used television to gauge the state of England's liver, you'd have booked it in for a transplant ages ago. Women in gutters, men fighting, men in gutters, women fighting, a nice old lady putting on a bandage, police, vomiting, more police, more vomiting, laughing, swearing and road sweepers clearing away the rubbish in the cold light of dawn. And that's it. You never see a programme where some people go out, have a nice evening and then go home again. So let us spend this chapter taking a less hyperbolic, more objective look at the English on a night out. Maybe we are as bad as we look on the telly. But maybe, Your Honour, we are not.

I'm afraid the case for the defence is not going to start well. We can dismiss *Party Paramedics* with the clink of a pint glass but we can't dismiss a BBC report quoting Mohantha Dooldeniya, a surgeon at Pinderfields Hospital in Wakefield. Mr Dooldeniya had operated on three women who had drunk so much that their bladders had exploded. He was evidently concerned at the binge-drinking culture that was keeping his operating table busy. He didn't actually say exploded. He said burst but it's pretty much the same thing, medically speaking.

Now. This wasn't the worrying bit. I'm not a woman and I've never been to Wakefield. The worrying bit came further into the story. Mr Dooldeniya went on to explain that he found the spike in female bladder explosions surprising because it's normally the men who burst first. Men have longer urethras, you see. We need more pressure to get the urine out. And we drink pints rather than spritzers.

The report did not reveal how many exploded men Mr Dooldeniya had stitched back up. It could have been four and they too could have all been from Wakefield. But that seems unlikely. Long urethras. More liquid. More pressure. It could be eight. Or ten. It might not even be a problem specific to Wakefield. Whatever the actual figure and geographical spread, news that we are now capable of drinking so much that our bladders rupture before we realise we need the loo feels like a line crossed, don't you think?

And then there's the brain damage. Some scientists got a group of rats drunk for two days. They didn't say in which town or during which happy hour this massive rodent bender took place but at the end of it, they didn't just have some very hung-over rats. They had rats with extensive degeneration in the entorhinal cortex of their brains. This sounds bad because it is. The entorhinal cortex is important. It has special responsibilities for our autobiographical and episodic memories. It's how we remember our names and house numbers. Does any of this ring any alarm bells? Have you been those rats? What on earth have we done to our entorhinal cortexes? Another line crossed.

This is usually the point where people gaze dreamily across the Channel and say, 'Ahhh, if only we could be more like the French.' And I say, 'Why?'

And they say, 'Because guess what? They drink with their meals. Isn't that amazing?'

It isn't just Marcel, our friend in his perfect Parisian office. It's all of them. Across the whole of France, daily, the following conversation takes place in absolutely every *lieu de travail.*

'Shall we have lunch, Pierre?'

'*Bien sûr*, Monsieur Bertillon.'

'Shall we just grab a sandwich from Pret and eat it at our desk really, really quickly?'

'*Non. Zut alors*.'

'Of course *non*. It was just my little joke. We are not animals. We are not zee English. Let us go to the café and eat vegetables and then meat on separate plates at separate times very, very slowly, taking care to chew each mouthful to enjoy the simple, yet delicious flavours while at the same time discussing EU agricultural subsidies, the outrageousness of having to work until we are fifty-eight and our other women. And let us drink wine with our nine-course lunch but in moderation to make our gastronomique experience all zee more civilised.'

'*Bon*.'

'*Bon.*'

'*Bien sûr.*'

'*On y va?*'

'*Oui.*'

Meanwhile, the French – based on their knowledge of Calais and *Party Paramedics* – think we're all binge-drinking animals. They blame us for ruining their Gallic traditions with our infectious, hellish drinking habits.

'The French kids are the worst because they want to be Anglo-Saxons,' Jean-Christophe, a Parisian waiter told the *Guardian* in a feature bemoaning the demise of the continental café culture. 'They start knocking back the strong beers early on and then move on to shots, often without eating. They know it's what the English do, and they think it's cool to be boisterous. The kids become so intoxicated that they vomit and urinate anywhere they can find, and they'll be up for a fight too. Pretty soon you have disturbances all over the area, and that's when the police arrive. It's not something we're used to in Paris.'

Now, there's a lot for which we can be held responsible. Cucumber sandwiches. Badminton. Roundabout sponsorship. Haggis.* But forcing the French to drink? *Non.* They drink more than us each year. They used to drink a lot more but they've been reining it in over the last fifty years, from the equivalent of 25 litres of pure alcohol per year in 1961 to a mere 13.67 now. We, on the other hand, were rather

* It is English, okay – look it up.

147

prim in 1961, sipping a very responsible seven litres. There's only so much Mateus Rosé a sixties swinger can drink. Now we're at 13.4, almost double. But still, crucially, less than the French. Yes, it's also true that we tend to chin it all in one epic night, probably in Wakefield. But is that really such a problem?

The French have higher rates of liver cirrhosis. And, to generalise criminally based on one night out in the Bastille fifteen years ago, their nightclubs are dreadful. Cheesy. Full of sharking men and bottom-pinched women. They do dinner well. We do drinking well. And this isn't a new phenomenon. People have been complaining about our boozing for millennia.

'In your dioceses, the vice of drunkenness is too frequent,' moaned the eighth-century missionary and supergrass St Boniface in a postcard to the Archbishop of Canterbury. 'Neither the Franks nor the Gauls nor the Lombards nor the Romans nor the Greeks commit it.' Not even the Greeks. Can you imagine? Just us and some Vikings getting hammered. In *Man Walks Into a Pub*, the author and beer aficionado Pete Brown lists 119 English colloquialisms for getting drunk, from the everyday arseholed, comatose, half-cut, smashed, shit-faced and twatted to the more specialist boohonged, blootered, gattered, jiggered, jagged, kaylied, roistered and, of course, ferschtinkenered. As in, 'I got completely ferschtinkenered last night. Ended up on a bus in Colchester with a cup of coffee. It was awesome.'

Mead in the monasteries.

Beer in the taverns.

Gin in the slums.

More beer.

More gin.

Le Piat d'Or.

Stella.

WKD.

This is English evolution. But it's no use just saying this. We have to prove it. Let us get to the heart/bladder of the matter. Let us start at the bladder-bursting daddy of them all: Wakefield on a Saturday night. I'm willing to bet you two large glasses of Pinot Grigio, get the rest of the bottle free, I don't burst a thing.

IN THE MIDDLE AGES, Wakefield was known as the 'Merrie City', undoubtedly because of its vibrant nightlife, its excellent array of cocktails and its beautiful women. Nothing has changed. It's one in the morning and I'm standing on a balcony in X Bar looking down at lots of beautiful women. They have clearly drunk an excellent array of cocktails. They also appear to be vibrant – luminous, even. I'm not going to do all of Wakefield Tourist Board's work for it. There are some unbeautiful women here as well. And men, lots of men, none of them beautiful at all. But it is, undoubtedly, a Very Merrie City.

Because it's still early, the unbeautiful men are trying to pick off the beautiful women with a combination of what I imagine they imagine are slick dance moves and comedy dance moves. Because the slick dance moves are not slick and the comedy dance moves aren't funny, they are struggling. One of the men, astonished at his lack of success, just goes in for a direct, desperate snog on a girl in a tangerine boob tube. He gets a slap for his trouble and returns to Plan A (big box, little box, big box, little box . . . and moon walk and repeat, two, three-four) in a different corner of the dance floor. Another man takes his place, opening with a smile and the sprinkler move. The girl with the tangerine boob tube is not amused.

I feel momentarily sorry for all these desperate men trying their luck in an environment from which we long ago should have evolved until I realise it's working. One by one, the women are being picked off, separated from their packs like wounded wildebeest. Some of them even have wounded-wildebeest limps. (Maybe the six-inch stilettos were a bad idea?) No exploding bladders though. None.

Out on the street, there are two police video vans, dozens of police officers and dozens more security guards. They're not taking any chances. I wander down to Fanny and Bacardi, the Ronseal of Wakefield nightclubs, but a bouncer notices my notebook as he waves in a group of six very drunk blokes.

'What's with the notebook, mate?'

I explain that I am just, you know, writing something about nightlife in England. We quickly agree that we don't need my sort round here and I would be better off taking my notebook elsewhere. So I go to Reflex where it's also all kicking off but in a good way.

'Happy birthday, Michelle,' shouts the DJ. Michelle screams. All Michelle's friends scream. The DJ plays the Spice Girls. Michelle screams again. Then Spandau Ballet. All her friends scream. It's quite grating to watch sober so I buy a line of brightly coloured shots off a roving shot-purveyor and down them. Some time later, I am dancing (big box, little box, still got it, yeah). Wakefield is fun. I love dancing.

Half-two and the main street now resembles a Roman piazza only colder, drunker and with kebab shops instead of pizzerias. The rose-sellers are doing a brisk trade. Romance is thick in the air. Romance and vomit. Romance, vomit and flying glass. Those wildebeest who weren't picked off earlier are propping each other up and laughing like hyenas which causes problems with my safari metaphor but is true. Everything is funny at 3 a.m. in Wakefield unless you're Simon and Geoff.

Simon and Geoff are Street Angels. I know this because it says so on the front of their high-vis jackets. I wait for them to bandage the hand of a man who has just been bottled before asking them what Street Angels do.

'We're volunteers,' says Geoff. 'We do first aid, help people out, try to take the pressure off the emergency services.' They're like the bus people in Colchester only they don't have a bus. Why would anyone volunteer to stand in the street every Saturday night patching up drunk people?

'It was better than just sitting around,' says Geoff, who first volunteered when he was unemployed.

Simon does it because he used to be on the other side. 'I used to be one of them,' he says, pointing at a very drunk man piggy-backing another very drunk man into a wall. 'Now it's time for me to give something back.'

'What have you had to deal with so far tonight?'

'Just that bloke with the cut hand. He got bottled in the bar over there. He put his hand up to protect his face so he's lucky.' Last week, they had to deal with a girl who fell off her heels and knocked herself out in the gutter. No burst bladders though. Not a single one. And then Geoff gets a message on his earpiece. CCTV has spotted a man failing to cross a road. No cars involved. No potholes. Just the man, his legs and several thousand pints of Carlsberg. Suspected concussion.

Geoff and Steve race off in one direction and I wander off in the other. I have one more thing to do before I can leave. I must eat a pie. Acting on a tip-off, I turn right up a side street, through a doorway, up two flights of stiletto-confounding stairs, through another doorway to the Wakefield Pie Shop.

'All right, love, what can I get you?'

'What's the speciality?' I don't know why I always go posh in a late-night pie shop. It's so annoying.

'Pie,' she replies, deadpan.

'May I have the pie, please?' Ridiculous. Just stop it. Talk normal.

'With peas?'

'Are they mushy?' Oh for goodness sake. Of course they're going to be mushy. You're not at Le Manoir aux Quat'Saisons.

'Yes, love.' I told you.

'No, thank you. Just the pie if it's possible.'

'With chips and beans?'

'Yes.'

'Four pounds, love.'

I'm not going to lie, it was the finest pie I've ever eaten. Actually, that was a bit of a lie. It was the pie that most exceeded my pie-based expectations. I had expected something as stringy as a tennis racket, as chewy as loft insulation made of horse hoof, cow knuckle, dog sinew and despair. But this was not that pie. It was deliciously seasoned, tender, slow-cooked, melt-in-the-mouth. The pastry would have impressed my grandmother and my grandmother knew about pastry. And horse racing. And biltong smuggling. But mainly pastry. If Wakefield really was the bladder-bursting capital of England, the pie would not need to be this good. They wouldn't need to bother.

On the way out, I pass Simon and Geoff and a man with blood streaming down his face. I pass a vomiter, another vomiter, five crying women, four fighting men, and two very large middle-aged people holding each other's crotches in a doorway. This is all very well but what else are people getting up to of an evening?

*   *   *

An estimated 2 million people play bingo in England and almost all of them are old. Now, one is aware that bingo does not have the coolest of reputations but 2 million wrinklies can't be wrong. Could it be that the only thing between the rest of us and England's greatest night out is ageism – and the unedifying image of a granny tonguing a grandpa because he just got a full house?

Around seven o'clock on a nondescript Tuesday deep in the Midlands, I phone Stockland Green Gala Bingo, 'Your value bingo club', and ask if I can rock up mid-evening, given that I hadn't had dinner and it's never nice gambling on an empty stomach.

'No, love,' says the woman. 'You have to be here by half seven. You don't want to miss the first session.'

I hail a taxi and tell the driver not to spare the horses.

'What?' says the taxi-driver.

'Nothing. Just, could you hoof it? I must get to the bingo in ten minutes.'

'The bingo?'

'Yes. I'm just, err, well, I've never, umm—'

'I love the bingo,' he interrupts. 'Crazy people. Brilliant fun.'

'What?'

The taxi-driver was not old. He was almost young. And he loved the bingo. This might be a pretty good evening after all.

Or not. Outside the bingo hall, two angry old women on mobility scooters are having a vicious argument. They are so angry, I can't understand what they're arguing about – something to do with cigarettes or men or poly-tunnels – so I step around them and a man with a very small head locked in a staring match with a Staffordshire bull terrier.

'You haven't done this before, have you?' asks the lovely lady at reception rhetorically, as she might if I was arriving for my first cage fight. 'Follow me.'

We walk past the fruit machines – fluffers for the main event – through double doors into a hall the size of half a football pitch. At least 200 people are arranged around cafeteria tables, staring in silence at portable screens or bits of paper. The lights are abattoir bright.

It is very quiet. You can hear the hum of the air-conditioning. If people are talking, it is in a whisper. Most sit in anticipatory silence. High above them, the high priestess of bingo looks out from her pulpit, preparing to start proceedings.

'Do you want a screen or paper?' asks the maternal receptionist, still chaperoning me.

'Umm.'

'Quick, because it's going to start.'

'Paper.'

'Right, here's your dabber.'

'My dabber?'

'Yes. For dabbing.'

I run to a table next to two women in pink cardigans who aren't talking and two other women in silver baseball caps who aren't talking. It is a library with nothingness instead of books.

Tracey Claire, the high priestess, begins. Her voice is soft and calm, ethereal, a bit TomTom. She was the runner-up in the national Caller of the Year competition 2008 no less, only the second competition she'd ever entered. In the interval, she will tell me she was the only woman in the final, that she suspects the media hype might have ruined her chances of winning, that she couldn't see what the (male) winner brought to the table. She will also tell me that she has seen OAPs fighting over lucky seats and that if you don't 'keep control of the room, things can change very, very quickly'. For now though, bingo!

'Green page everyone. Double bubble.' It's such a strange atmosphere, halfway between a funeral in a basketball hall and a well-organised cult preparing to go out with a bang.

'Eyes down, ladies and gentlemen,' says Tracey. 'One and four, fourteen. Three and two, thirty-two. All the fours, forty-four . . .' The pace is relentless. I'm dabbing with my dabber but it's almost impossible to keep up. I glance around and the silver baseball cappees are texting with one hand and dabbing with the other. I imagine the part of their brain that deals with number-spotting is a great throbbing lump of over-exercised grey matter.

'Four and nine, forty-nine.'

From the other side of the room, there's a half-hearted, 'Yep.'

A communal groan of frustration or jealousy or outright hatred ripples through the rest of the hall as Tracey confirms the win. 'And that's a valid claim.'

'One thousand pounds pays for Christmas,' explains the manager after the first game is over. 'Five thousand is life-changing. Some of these in here, they're extremely savvy. They're pound clever.'

'Five and four, fifty-four . . .'

As Tracey continues her hypnotic roll call of random numbers, I don't get the impression anyone's actually enjoying themselves. The professionals are filling out two paper lines and two computer lines at the same time, totally focused, totally incapable of making small talk. And then there are the stares, the bingo stares, like Clint Eastwood just before he goes for his gun. They grow more hostile as the evening wears on and the opportunities to win decrease. No one celebrates when someone shouts, 'Full house.'

'For those of you staying, it's time for party bingo,' says Tracey. I'm not staying. As Stockland Green links up with Wolverhampton, Rotherham and other hushed bingo cathedrals full of bug-eyed dabbers in baseball caps, I leave. It turns out 2 million old people can be wrong.

'LIVERPOOOWELLL. Thahchhs whirr isaaaacht,' said my Liverpudlian friend, and yes, I apologise for my accent. In a straw poll of English cities, Liverpool comes out top for nightlife. This is not just a straw poll of Liverpudlians. It's a straw poll of straw polls. Liverpool is always voted top in best nightlife surveys. Everyone I asked who would know agreed. The cars-on-bricks stereotype, the Harry Enfield fighting shell suits . . . all out of date. Liverpool is glamorous, sophisticated, whirr isaaaacht.

Within minutes of arriving, it's obvious it's at here, where I am. Even before I arrive, I know I am at where it is. Even the toll booth attendant for the Queensway Tunnel (I got lost en route) is an immaculate Scouser – intricate make-up, manicured nails, big, big hair. Confidence. Beauty. Wit. A desire to make something of life. I may have read too much into our brief encounter. Toll booths are not designed for conversation.

The last time I was in Liverpool they'd only done the docks. These relics of different greatness had been regenerated into a restaurant quarter with pedestrian areas, boutiques and, kill me now, a Beatles experience. In the intervening few years, the regeneration has spread up from the Mersey into town. Liverpool is now a vast glass multiplex of interwoven arcades climbing up to Hope Street. There are cinemas and hotels and galleries and intimidating designer shops selling £100 T-shirts, £350 trainers and Moncler fur-lined children's ski suits for £400. And there are hair salons, my God, there are hair salons. At the Barbara Daley salon, a favourite of wags and wagettes and wagettes-in-waiting, hair is everything and today, a Friday, the atmosphere is electric (in a good way, not in a static, hair-standing-on-end way). The weekend is here and the full smorgasbord of hair pampering is on the menu. You can have permanent waves, Xtenso partial smoothing, highlights, lowlights, a root regrowth tint, a calming and repairing facial treatment, lavish lashes, shellac nails, an algomask, a tan, an eyebrow tint, an eyelash perm, a facial wax, a lip wax, a back wax, a Hollywood, a Brazilian or a haircut. Cameron, the creative director ('it means I'm more experienced . . . and older') has been doing blow-dries and hair extensions all day. She's exhausted.

'How much do extensions cost?' I ask, a tiny bit tempted because I've always wanted to go the full Axl Rose but never got past the bouffant phase.

'Oh my goodness. It can vary. People pick them up really, really cheaply,' she says disapprovingly. 'You can get them in Primark for £10 and stick them in your hair yourself. They look horrendous. Or you get them here and it's upwards of £1,000.'

'Wow.'

'It's instant volume, very Americanised. I've been in Liverpool for eight years and it was already the thing when I started. But each year, the city just gets more and more glamorous. People are spending huge amounts of money to go out. We've just had a fifteen-year-old girl in and she's had the works. Some ladies come in twice a week, maybe for a blow dry on a week day if they're going out to a nice dinner and then again for the weekend. It's all about big hair. Big hair and high heels.'

'It doesn't sound very, well, you know, feminist.'

'Oh no. Not here. Here, the men are men. The women are women. It's an eye-opener. Are you going out tonight?'

Of course I'm going out tonight. A club crawl, taking in all the finest venues in Liverpool and therefore England, starting at San Carlo for aperitivos, moving on to Alma de Cuba for salsa, swinging by Mosquito because it will be 'pumping', avoiding Fanny and Bacardi because they don't have one here, and finishing at Playground.

We needn't dwell on the details except to say that by the time I arrive at Playground, I have feathers in my hair, glitter wedged in the back of my eyes, blisters, a headache and a sense that I got the wrong night. I have this sense because the second thing everyone has said all night is, 'You got the wrong night, mate.'

The first thing everyone said was, 'All right, mate?' delivered in the way everyone else might say, 'Have you got a problem, mate?' It's not just the tone, it's the body language that goes with it. Very direct. Full-frontal. Aggressively welcoming, like the Maoris shot by Captain Cook (world's worst diplomat) when he first dropped anchor off New Zealand.

Once I had established they weren't going to head-butt me, I found my fellow clubbers to be full of the joys of their city. I can't think of anywhere else in England except perhaps Ironbridge and Chipping Sodbury where the locals are quite so passionate about their home town.

'Best place in the world, eh?'

'Are you enjoying it? Are ya? Well, are ya? Eh? Eh?'

'Better than London, isn't it? Eh?'

'Don't you think it's a thousand times better than London? You see, people up here are genuine.'*

'You should be here tomorrow. It's going to be massive, mate.'

It's not that it's quiet. It's just not quite as glamorous and wild and vajazzled as everyone, absolutely bloody everyone, says it will be tomorrow. And then I get to Playground, the £500-a-year members' bar recently opened at the Hilton Hotel. This is the place where your Coleens, Abbeys and Alexes hang out. Alex Gerrard, Stylish Scouser of the Year nominee and wife of Stevie, even designed the membership card. It's also the place where a 'young financier' made national headlines in 2012 after splashing out £125,000 on one bottle of champagne. It was a big bottle – thirty litres – but it's been a while since any bankers down south have dared to do that. Tonight, though, the place is empty.

'It's empty,' I say to the beautiful hostess who has ushered me to my table.

'It's still early,' she says. 'And you've come on the wrong night. Tomorrow's going to be—'

'Yes, I know.'

I wait around, a wallflower on the edge of a tumbleweed

---

* It should be footnoted, which is why it is, that Liverpudlians (a) complain a lot about how they are unfairly stereotyped and (b) do an awful lot of stereotyping themselves. For example, I have met at least five Londoners who are completely genuine.

dance floor. A group arrives. Three glittery women looking thoroughly unhappy at their impractical choice of foot-wear and . . . is that? No. It can't be. It is. In the flesh. Bobby Davro. That's how glamorous Liverpool can be.

WHEN I WAS YOUNG and single and happy and flat-sharing in west London, my flatmates and I would dine out at a curry house once, twice and occasionally three times a week.

Chicken madras, pilau rice, £5.20. 'Hello, Mr Matt, we made it extra-spicy.'

For three years, I tried to convince them it was too spicy. Three painful, beautiful years. And then the curry house became a gastro-café serving beetroot soup and elderflower ice cream. This would never happen in Birmingham's Balti Triangle.

Jav, my Kashmiri taxi-driver, 'born and bred in Brum', resplendent in Gandalf beard and white robes, is having none of it. 'I don't know why everyone gets so excited about the balti,' he says. 'It's only a little metal bowl.' Explaining to a Kashmiri how curry night is an English institution seems a bit ridiculous. He knows it anyway. He always has people in the back of his taxi, looking for Britain's best curry. He's just winding me up.

'That place you've got there,' he continues. 'That's not even the best balti house, man. I don't trust that one at all. You want to go to my cousin's place.'

'I can't tell you how many taxi-drivers have told me I should go to their cousin's place,' I point out.

'No, no, no, no, no, no, no. I promise you, it's great, man. It's where all the taxi-drivers go. It's on the way. I'll show you.'

'It's going to be rubbish. Cousins' places always are.'

'No, man, seriously, trust me . . .'

So Jav and I pull up outside his cousin's place twenty-five curry houses short of the one Google swears is best. It looks dark and empty and very unlike the finest balti house in Birmingham. Jav versus Google. Google looks like it wins.

'Thanks, Jav. It looks great.' I'm lying but I don't want to offend him. He's not offended. He's worried.

'No, man, the good chef's not in,' he says, peering through the window. 'That's his son. I don't trust that one. He's a bit of a joker.'

'I don't mind. I'm sure it will be—' He's already inside, chatting with the joker, demanding to know what he's cooking and how. Then he's out again, shaking his head and we're off down Ladypool Road, cousin's gaff rejected, the meter long since switched off.

'This is the place. Look.' Behold Lahore Village. And it's packed. 'I can go in and check,' says Jav.

'No, it's fine. This looks great.'

'Here's my number. If it's no good, call me.'

Oh. My. God. You have to go. Just for the vegetable pakora starter. Not the burgers, they didn't look so good even though practically every other person in the place was eating them.

For my main course, I stuck to plan A. I had the chicken karahi and it arrived, as advertised, in an unassuming little metal bowl, spiced and warm, deep red with fresh coriander and a garlic naan. '*The genuine and authentic food service here has been created with an exotic collection of herbs distinctively blended in the traditional ways of the Punjab and Northwest frontier of Pakistan . . . to give you delight dishes to touch the tastebuds,*' boasts the menu. My taste buds were touched. I crossed the road for a mango lassi and phoned Jav.

'It was brilliant, man.'

'Yes! You've made my night. Shall I come and pick you up?'

'Thank you.'

CURRY BEATS LIVERPOOL on the wrong night beats Wakefield pie beats bingo. And despite the exhaustive research (I hope you're grateful), my bladder is intact and my liver only shivers in the morning. But of course, we haven't even set foot in the most important of English institutions, the place where drinking has always been done, the place where the *Party Paramedics* are not needed. We haven't set foot in the old man's pub. Our last stop in the quest to find joy and love and maybe some sozzled hugging? The old man's pub, of course. And, because we're not doing things by lemonade-topped halves in this chapter, we are off to the oldest old man's pub of all.

The Ye Olde Trip to Jerusalem, one of several pubs claiming to be the oldest in England, has a gift shop, a free, downloadable iPhone app and a sign in the main bar, resplendent in medieval font, that reads: '*You can find us on Facebook*.' Before we judge, let us consider what this pub has been through to survive more than eight centuries in the caves under Nottingham Castle. In 1194, for example, Prince John, errant brother of the crusading Richard I, besieged the castle, fought a battle and took it. Then Richard I came back from holiday and took it back. In 1330, for another example, Edward III staged a coup d'état against his mum, Isabella of France, and her lover, Roger Mortimer. In 2007, for another example still, smoking was banned in all the pubs of England. Five thousand pubs closed in the five years after the new legislation. Blood bath, albeit a healthy one. Those pubs that have survived have to compete with cut-price alcohol in the supermarkets and cut-price Wetherspoons. So of course some of them are going to have a Facebook page. And a gift shop. And a gastronomic menu. With bison burgers and fig chutney and crusty bread and aioli.

Despite the splash of Disneyfication, this is still a tremen-dous pub. There are snugs and nooks all over the place. The beer is perfectly kept. My pint of Legend smells of wet dog, wet horse and wet bracken and it tastes of a cosy jumper on a foggy day. There is no piped music, no James Blunt telling us we're beautiful when we quite evidently are not. There is no WKD. Well, there is but no one is drinking it. Well, they are but most of us are on the wet dog. It's six on a Saturday and it's packed with grumpy old men, middle-aged couples and students dressed as Daleks (what japes!). There are tourists, of course, here to tick Ye Oldest Pub box but they're getting much more than a tick in a box. They're seeing our culture at its most unassuming, uneventful and glorious. A pub. A pint. A fireside chat about nothing much in particular. And no girls in gutters or boys fighting. Or burst bladders.

The couple sitting at the table next to mine are Spanish. They are examining their half pints of bitter like a vet examines a particularly nasty case of ringworm. I smile at them and nod warmly, delighted to share this great moment with them.

They nod back and smile. Without meaning to, I have forced their hand. They're going to have to sip the bitter or the Englishman might be offended. I've been in this situation with sheep eyeballs in Azerbaijan, rotten shark meat in Iceland and still-furry-but-barbecued guinea pig in Peru. I don't feel too sorry for them.

He sips first. She follows. They show no reaction at all which is international for, 'Bleurrgghhh'.

I go to the toilet. When I come back, they've ordered a nice, crisp bottle of rosé. We exchange smiles again and in that moment of international harmony, where we have agreed to disagree, I feel proud of the English pub and its wet dog on tap. I might even celebrate with a packet of pork scratchings.

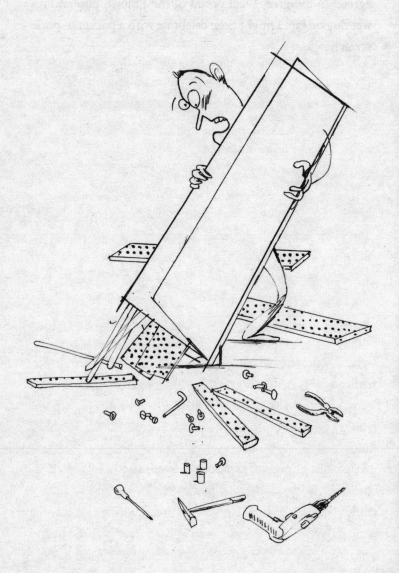

THE SHOPS

And I am a weapon of massive consumption,
And it's not my fault it's how I'm programmed to function.

LILY ALLEN, poet

WE HAVE A SUBPRIME MORTGAGE. We have a leaking roof. We have a terminally ill boiler and an oven with only two temperature settings: nothing or slightly hotter than the Earth's core. We have many other pressing financial obligations, not helped by the thieving car insurance people, the thieving electricity people and the thieving children. So far, so typical. But what do I only go and do late one night on the internet when I should have been innocently surfing niche pornography or chatting with my future Thai bride? I order a Championship Football Table for many hundreds of pounds.

I don't know how Wife has resisted the urge to say, 'Why the hell did you spend many hundreds of pounds on a goddam football table when you claimed we didn't have enough money to hire a professional wasp nest remover or buy fruit or go on holiday anywhere other than Wales in anything other than a tent?' Maybe she sensed that the purchase was psychologically significant for a man whose shed fell down.* Maybe she really likes table football. Maybe she's having an affair. Whatever it is, she let it go with an entirely ambiguous, 'You bought a football table.'

Some weeks later, the table arrived, right in the dying embers of an unfeasibly wide delivery window, and it was flat-packed. Now, let me be clear: my heart did not sink. I was in no way concerned. As we have discussed, I have long ago abandoned my opposition to flatpackery. We live in the Epoch of IKEA with its Billies and its filthy, delicious, so-this-is-what-early-onset-rigor-mortis-feels-like hot dogs.** I am down with the flat pack.

The Championship Football Table wasn't from IKEA, and it's only when you get flatpackery from another company that you realise how perfect, how honed, how economical the IKEA experience has become. I got the legs on. I got

---

* Yes, add that to the list. Fallen-down shed. Can't buy a new one because no ordinary shed seems appropriate without a Polynesian thatch or a massive television. And unless a lot of people read this book, that's not going to happen any time soon.

** Yes, yes, I know. This is the second mention of IKEA hot dogs and we're only halfway through, but I don't see why they should be brought down because a batch of their meatball colleagues had horse in them and they are still the best way in the world to spend 50p. If IKEA was sex, the hot dog would be the post-coital cigarette. IKEA is not sex.

the goals on. I got the little men on. I adjusted the bolts. I connected the struts. I lined up the final, structurally critical supporting crossbar. But then, crunch. The last screw went crooked and split out of the wood. And suddenly I was experiencing the flat-pack equivalent of Devon Loch doing the splits on the final furlong of the 1956 Grand National.

'Hi, your table arrived this morning,' I emailed the company charmingly. 'As you will see from the photo, the last horizontal strut has split when I was putting it together. The table itself seems good quality but the strut has failed. Are you able to send a replacement strut? I'm obviously reluctant to break down and repackage the whole table.'

I got an immediate reply. It told me that my email was very important to the company and that it would reply very soon.

Two days passed.

Then another day.

Then Ryan emailed to offer his sincerest apologies for the disappointment I must have felt upon this damage occurring which, he pointed out, was even more frustrating for them knowing that they did try to control 100 per cent of the products when they left the manufacturer and again when they went through their UK warehouse.

'Of course, if you would like us to come and collect the item from you and issue you with a full refund then we would be happy to do so, knowing however that you will have to repack the item and wait home on the day that HDNL come and collect from you.'

This was Ryan's Plan A but he also had a Plan B.

'We can also collect the product and arrange that a replacement is sent out to you as soon as one is available. Unfortunately this can sometimes mean a wait for the replacement to arrive in the UK.'

Now. If I'm honest, I wasn't keen on Plan A or Plan B. Trying to repack flatpackery is all but impossible, particularly if the polystyrene and cardboard packaging has disintegrated on unpacking (back off, I was excited). But as if Ryan had read my mind, he had a Plan C *and* a Plan D as well.

'I appreciate that this may not be the best possible scenario, so there are two other options I'd like to propose to you.'

Go on, Ryan. I'm all ears. 'You could keep the football table as is with a £60 refund on your order or you could keep it with a £75 voucher valid on any future order of any amount.'

Hmm. I like your style, young man, I really do. A bit of a cash sweetener to get things moving. You've been watching *The Apprentice*. The problem is, Ryan, that the football table cost many hundreds of pounds and £60, while not to be sniffed at, doesn't really make up for the fact that the table will collapse if we ever decide to use it. Moreover, Ryan old chum, an extra fifteen quid to be obliged into future transactions with your company is not going to tip the balance either, not when my relationship with your company is already under some considerable strain.

'Again, please accept my apologies for the disappointment and trouble that this must have caused you,' Ryan continued, showing a remarkable degree of empathy. 'I hope that we are able to help rectify this situation in a way that you are happy with.'

'Dear Ryan,' I emailed back, because it is both traditional and constructive to be polite with customer service representatives. 'Please can you just deliver a replacement strut.'

I got an immediate response. My email was important to the company and it would reply as soon as possible.

I'm sorry to have to tell you this but that was the last I heard from Ryan. I emailed again. That email was also important to them but not important enough to spark the impetus to reply. I emailed again and again. Finally I got Sammi who didn't know what had happened to Ryan but reiterated how keen they were to find a solution. Sammi's Plan A was strikingly similar to Ryan's. She would arrange collection of the faulty table and then send a replacement. I just needed to dismantle the table, repackage it and wait in for a day for the collection and another day for the second delivery. There was no Plan B. Sammi was obviously from the Rambo school of customer service.

'If you need to purchase packaging materials to do this you can always scan the receipt for them and I can pay back the cost for this.'

'Dear Samantha,' I replied, still being polite but you'll note I've gone with the formal 'Samantha' as per her email signature rather than 'Sammi' as per her very annoying sign-off. This is my way of registering that this is serious, that we are on a collision course, that I don't have a machine to scan a receipt.

'Weeks ago, I asked if you could send a replacement strut which would save you money and me time. Your alternative, to send a whole new table and expect me to repackage the damaged one, seems crazy. Either sending a replacement strut or attempting to repackage it yourselves (good luck with that) are the only practicable options.'

I got an immediate response. My email was important to it. It would reply as soon as possible.

Two days later, Sammi replied. She couldn't take the strut from the replacement table and just send that because of the delivery company and the warehouse and the remaining uncertainties surrounding the origins of our species and the dog had eaten her homework and it's a different department and Germany always wins on penalties. She couldn't even have the replacement table delivered and let me switch struts because the delivery company wouldn't wait. She was really sorry.

'If you would like a full refund please let me know and I will be happy to arrange that for you. In this case, to save the hassle of collection you can keep the item and either reuse it or discard it at your own discretion.'

What? Sorry? A full refund *and* I keep the table?

Yup. Plan G.

Welcome to online shopping. It has its pros and cons.

The main disadvantage, other than the simple fact that when England was a nation of shopkeepers you could take your football table back to the shopkeeper you bought it from and complain to his actual face, is that online shopping is killing Christmas. On Christmas Day 2012, Britons spent 17 million hours shopping online. Not each. It isn't that bad. But still, that's more than an hour per household. The idea that we spend all morning unwrapping stuff, then stuff our faces with stuff, then spend all afternoon buying more stuff is NOT VERY APPEALING. Christmas Day should be a time for love, happiness, alcohol, daytime snoring, *ET* and simmering family tensions.* Not bloody shopping.

The main advantage is obvious. You don't have to go to the shops.

SATURDAY AFTERNOON at the Bullring, Birmingham's futuristic shopping centre, already nine years old so perhaps not that futuristic any more. From the outside, it is reassuringly different from your average mall, curvaceous and shimmering like a large blob of mercury though not as toxic. I walk up and down steps to get in, actually quite excited. Well, not excited but ambivalent which is much

---

* A 2007 study found that 8 January is the busiest day of the year for divorce lawyers. The other peak is just after the summer holidays. In short, we get on better when we aren't together.

better than usual. My ambivalence is short-lived. Inside, it is less like a large blob of mercury and more like a shopping centre in that it is a three-storey-high building full of shops. Very light and airy though.

The thing that strikes you immediately is that almost all these shops are selling saucy underwear. Maybe it wouldn't strike you. Maybe that's normal to you. Maybe shopping centres are now very much focused on the purveying of crotchless panties, maybe window displays of French dancing girls are de rigueur – and I just missed that particular shopping-centre trend. Maybe I just got trapped in the lingerie cluster. But there's Ann Summers here, La Senza there, Boux Avenue over there.* None of the couples, families or dirty old men perusing the many racks of naughty lingerie seems perturbed. They are behaving as if they are in River Island or JoJo Maman Bébé.

'Look at this here, Nigel. Do you like this Fantine black and pink tutu?'

'Not sure, Sandra, love. I think the Hollywood Cami Suspender would suit you better. A bit more, you know, mysterious.'

'Really, Nigel? It's a bit conservative.'

---

* Boux Avenue is a lingerie company launched by Theo Paphitis. 'I once had a chance meeting with a beautiful French girl, with an even more beautiful name – Boux,' says the Dragon. 'I knew there must be something in it – and when I was creating the brand it seemed to evoke and capture the right feeling.' Wherever Boux is today, she must be so ~~creeped out~~ proud.

'You might be right, Sandra. But you don't want to get cold, do you?'

'Oh, it's so difficult, Nigel. I just can't decide. Can you stand here for an hour in this cloying heat conforming to stereotype while I just try it on anyway?'

'Of course, Sandra, petal.'

It is so busy. This is what the people of the Midlands do these days. They work like the rest of us, they go to the pub like the rest of us, they watch telly, potter in the garden, all the usual stuff. And then, come the weekend, they buy naughty pants together.

And have their teeth whitened.

'Afternoon, sir, would you like to have your teeth whitened today?'

Nothing can give a man a bigger complex than a pretty girl with very white teeth suggesting, in public, that you might be the perfect candidate for impromptu emergency teeth whitening.

'I'm fine thanks,' I reply with a thin smile.

'It takes just ninety minutes to smile with confidence.'

'I've got some naughty pants to buy. I'll just take a leaflet.'

'*A brighter, whiter smile. Instant amazing results! Zero sensitivity – Zero Pain. Listen to music with our fab headset lights. Fast. Safe. Pleasant. Effective.*'

They've got 14,000 happy customers. Doesn't say how many unhappy ones.

On the top floor, away from the lingerie and the girl with the teeth, I take stock. Every city has one of these glass and aluminium superstructures – Liverpool, Bristol, Birmingham, Manchester, Wakefield, Exeter, Portsmouth – full of light and space and screaming credit cards. They aren't 'out-of-town' like Bluewater or the MetroCentre, they're right in the middle. The Westfield, which opened in 2011 in Stratford, is now the largest urban shopping centre in Britain. It 'offers 175,000 square metres of retail space', which makes it, hold on while I grab a calculator, seventeen times larger than Britain's largest cathedral.

Do we need to worry about this? People have been flogging things at the Bull Ring centuries before it became the Bullring. And it's not as if cathedrals aren't selling something either. Roll up, roll up, get your life ever after here. Forgiveness. Redemption. Water and wine (buy one get one free).

I walk out of the throbbing ball of mercury and pants to a quiet park and, quite unexpectedly, the 300-year-old St Philip's Cathedral. It has its own wow-factor: Corinthian columns, baroque flashes, stained-glass windows that would not have survived German bombers in the Second World War if they hadn't been secreted away by concerned parishioners. The boys' choir is mid-rehearsal. Their sound fills the nave so much more dramatically than Rihanna filled the shopping centre. It is clear, precise, the opposite of the background cacophony in the city around it. Even the silences between verses are thick and velvety. After an afternoon in the material world, the peacefulness of this spiritual one is overwhelming. This isn't because of any divine presence. It's because there's hardly anyone here. There's me, a deacon, a woman, two tramps and the choir. It is soothing.

And then the two tramps start chatting loudly, then arguing about the pros and cons of taxing the super-rich. The woman shushes them. The deacon then starts praying, possibly that he won't have to step in. Even if the woman starts a fight to the death with the tramps, it's still comparatively relaxing. God vs lingerie in the battle for our attention on a Saturday afternoon? Lingerie wins hands down. There will be a rematch on Sunday and lingerie will win that too.

'AND NOW SOME MESSAGES from our sponsors . . . Pauline Quirk Academy of Performing Arts opens in Barnsley on Saturday. The Pauline Quirk Academy. Be yourselves. Be amazing . . . The Taste of India, established in 1987. We were the first Indian restaurant in Penistone. Book now on Barnsley 766 951 . . . Hello, good morning, ladies and gentlemen. It's nine in the a. of the m. and you're listening to Penistone FM. Stay tuned for our discussion on dialects and, coming up, the ever delightful Noreen will be testing us on our 1930s confectioneries. But for now, let's pick up the tempo with Cher and the "Shoop Shoop Song".'

Cities can cope but what about market towns? How can they navigate the rise of the superstore? For a long time, doomsayers have been predicting the death of the high street, skewered on the three-pronged fork of supermarkets, out-of-town shopping centres and the internet. Is it dead? Is it dying? Or has it just got a mild dose of man flu?

Penistone,* South Yorkshire, is typical of a thousand market towns up and down the country. There's a butcher, a baker, never a candlestick maker when you need one.** There is a pub and there is another pub that has been dolled up with leather sofas and chrome bar taps, and now serves not only beer but thirteen different types of flavoured latte including, brace yourselves, honeycomb, cinnamon, chocolate mint and cranberry. There is a town hall and a pharmacist, a community centre, a train station: what more could you want?

Everything was ticking along quite uneventfully until Tesco applied for permission to open a superstore right in the very heart of town. This was a big deal, the biggest perhaps since the railway arrived in 1874 (King George and Queen Mary passed through the town centre in 1912 but they didn't stop so this was bigger than that). Many people were opposed. A pressure group was formed. 'Penistone is

---

* No, it's not pronounced like that. Penis comes from the Welsh Celtic 'penn' meaning head and 'is' meaning below, not the English 'penis' meaning penis. Welcome to the town below the hill. Not the town of penises.

** High-street candlestick manufacturers are few and far between. If you insist, I can recommend Price's, 43 Clarks Village, Street, Somerset, established in 1830 and once the largest candle manufacturer in the world. Good candles too.

a market town not a supermarket town,' they declared quite neatly. 'If we are not careful we will end up with one big store that would be better suited to the south-east than a Pennine market town.'

For years, the community resisted but Tesco did what it does best and kept reapplying and reapplying and re-applying. Eventually Barnsley council gave the final planning permission and construction began. The disruption was immense. Sue Lockwood, a local resident, said, 'I tried to get to my hairdresser on Wednesday. I ended up climbing over heaps of rubble, in my good shoes, while some man in a hard hat looked on and sniggered.'

The store opened two years ago which means enough time has passed for it to have killed the high street.

'Has Tesco killed your high street?' I ask two old ladies walking up the hill.

'Sorry, love?'

'Tesco. Has it killed your high street?'

'I don't think so. We were opposed to it though, weren't we?'

'Yes, we were but I quite like it.'

'It means we don't have to go to another town for things they don't have in the Co-op.'

'Yes, yes, but the high street,' I ask. 'Is it dead?'

'I still get my meat from Paul Schofield, the butcher.'

'Right. But I bet you're on your way to Tesco now.'

'No, we're going to Pilates.'

'Sorry?'

Paul Schofield, the butcher, is on holiday in Lanzarote so I ask the butcher's mate, Daniel, 'Has Tesco killed the high street?'

'I don't think so,' he replies.

'Are you sure?' I ask. 'Are you sure it's not dead?'

'If anything, business is better since Tesco opened. We've had people we've never seen before coming in. They pop in to Tesco and then come here for their meat.'

The pharmacist has noticed a change. The baby ranges don't sell well any more. 'But it's not the end of the world.' It might be if Tesco get permission to open a pharmacy. They keep applying but have, to date, been refused.

'Are we witnessing the death of a high street?' I ask a man coming out of the pub-pub, the one that doesn't do thirteen lattes.

'Sorry?'

'The death of the high street. Tesco. You know.'

'I bought some oven chips from Tesco yesterday,' he replies. 'I didn't realise that you had to freeze them so I'm keeping them in the fridge.'

'Okay.'

'What do you think?'

'I don't know. It doesn't seem like the high street has died.'

'No, the chips. Do you think they'll be okay?'

'Oh, umm. Yes. But what about the high street?'

'What high street?'

*   *   *

MAYBE THE HIGH STREET won't die. Some independent, specialist shops are adapting and surviving. At my local butcher, I can get air-dried zebra biltong and a whole sheep complete with Scout-built roasting machine. Try turning up at Tesco with that sort of shopping list. In 2011 there were 2,500 more independent shops than there were the year before. In 2012, the trend slowed but continued. Chain shops are vanishing. One-offs aren't. Market towns have become supermarket towns but some are trying to become market towns again.

Sixty miles north as the crow flies from Penistone, many, many more by road, is Hudswell, Very North Yorkshire, a one-horse village that has found a very different way to survive the tidal wave of supermarkets. The only shop in the village shut thirty years ago as its newly automotive customers deserted it for the nearest town of Richmond. And then in 2010 it opened again, across the road and smaller. Much smaller. The Little Shop, run by a committed rota of seventeen volunteering residents, is the smallest shop in England, a bonsai three metres squared. It doesn't sell bonsai. There isn't space. But it does manage to sell pretty much everything you need to avoid schlepping to Richmond in the car.

When I arrive, it is closed – an inconvenience store. So is the pub to which it is attached. If I were a local, I would have known the opening times but I'm not so I go for a stroll down a precipitous hill and struggle up it again by which time Stella has arrived with a cold but a determination to open on time.

'Hello,' she says.

'Afternoon,' I reply. That's the sort of friendliness you get when you go local.

'It started with the pub really,' she explains. 'It closed a few years ago, not because it was doing badly, but because the people who bought it paid too much for it. It just shut overnight. Three years later, someone suggested we all get together and buy the pub. So we did. We set up a committee and we bought it – Yorkshire's first community pub.'

The shop was the next natural step. It is the sort of shop children want to build when they play shops – straight-forward, old-school, a miniature Open All Hours (but not, as we've established, open all hours). There are no BOGOFs, no half-price wines or crisps or razorblades, no tiles that get smaller to make your trolley click over them faster so you push it slower when you're walking past expensive items.* It appears to be entirely free from subliminal messaging, hypnosis or marketing trickery. It appears to be just a village shop.

---

* Fifty-nine per cent of the stuff you buy in a supermarket is un-planned. Professor Alan Penn of University College London suggests you should 'go around the periphery of the supermarket first to pick up essential purchases.' Or start in the frozen aisle to give your shop a more urgent, supermarket-sweep-style emphasis. Or just accept that you are too weak to resist.

'One in the eye for the supermarkets, eh?' I say as Stella blows her nose.

'Well, most people still do a big shop in the supermarket and they just use us for day-to-day things. Mind you, the prices are fairly competitive. They're not bad in comparison. And we have a lot of local produce. These cards are done by the treasurer's sister-in-law, these are local biscuits, local eggs, local ice cream, Black Sheep ale . . .'

We pause as someone pops in to buy some bread.

'Afternoon,' says Stella.

'Hello, Stella,' says Someone. How civilised. Stella plays shop two hours a week for free. Some people do an hour, some do four. There are no perks. The person who does four hours doesn't get a better staff discount than the person who only does one.

'No, nothing like that,' says Stella. 'We get nothing in return. We're just providing a facility for people and they use it. A village has to have a pub and a shop, doesn't it? I think the pub is more important, to be honest. But the shop comes second.'

ACCORDING TO A 'non-scientific' survey in the *Wall Street Journal*, Americans now spend $1.2 trillion a year on stuff they don't need. This is a lot. Or, more specifically, 11 per cent of total consumer spending, which is 9 per cent higher than it was in 1959. We're not much better. Since the world went subprime, the balance has shifted a little from 'discretionary' spending to 'essential' spending. We're spending a little more on carrots and heating and a little less on revolutionary abdominisers. But this is not necessarily because we are becoming more chastened. It's because carrots and heating are more expensive than they used to be.

Each year, we spend more than £2 billion on kitchen gadgets we don't use. I have conducted a survey of my own kitchen drawers and found the following never-used items: a melon baller, a lettuce knife, a lettuce dryer, an olive pitter, an electric knife sharpener, an unelectric knife sharpener, an electric whisk, an electric cheese-grater, a tray that makes ice cubes shaped like lemons, two novelty potato mashers, three different garlic-peeling machines (none of which is necessary given that I now employ the Jamie Oliver-trademark bang-the-whole-bulb-in-sorted method), and an egg slicer because who, seriously, thinks it is quicker to find the egg slicer than to cut the goddam egg with the knife that's right goddam there? I hate all these gadgets. My life would be happier without them. In fact, I've now thrown them all out. Thank you, book.

Still, there are many worse things than a melon baller. You can buy electric nail files, electric candles, fondue sets and foot spas. You can buy a desk vacuum cleaner powered by a USB cable connected to your laptop. You can buy a plastic dog that poos green gunk and is marketed as 'educational'. You can and do spend £59 on a wristband that provides 'a personal energy system that helps bring your whole being into a state of balance where your body is stronger, your thoughts clearer and your endurance levels increased'. No, it doesn't.

You can also buy a 3D TV. I did. I was only in the shop for a toaster but the man said it was the future.

'It will transform your viewing experience.'

'Won't it be a bit much?'

'No way. It'll be like the monsters are in your living room.'

'That's what I mean.'

'Have you seen *Avatar*?'

'No.'

'Americans had to have counselling because they missed being in the *Avatar* forest.'

'I don't want people in blue body-stockings in my living room.'

'Okay, but look how clear the picture is.'

To be crystal clear in forty-inch surround-sound high-definition, 3D isn't the future unless the future involves wearing socially compromising goggles while feeling sick because things on the telly keep leaping out at you because the film director got a bit too excited about the new format.

And even if it was the future, it will soon become the past. That's the way it is with discretionary shopping. New becomes old. Cool becomes square. Must-have becomes must-put-in-the-attic becomes must-take-to-the-dump. Nowhere is this more apparent than at the Nevendon Giant Boot Sale, Essex – the 'longest established boot sale, running since 1989!'. At half past six on a Sunday morning, when you would quite reasonably expect Essex to be in bed, sleeping off all the excesses of the last chapter, the place is packed. Two huge fields contain row after row after row of hardcore booters. Some are wearing fur-lined gilets and have come in twelve-plate black-windowed Range Rovers. Others are wearing tattoos and have come in cars you normally see being confiscated for not having valid insurance in *Traffic Cops*. Every boot is yawning wide open, burping life's rejected contents out onto the trampled grass. The punters picking through this material bile would fill a thousand identity parades: haggling Poles, magpie-eyed Indians, camel-coated Essex Boys wheeling, dealing, attempting to charm the sellers another fifty pence lower. Speed is of the essence and if you close your eyes and imagine a particularly civilised episode of the *Antiques Roadshow*, perhaps set in the grounds of an abbey in West Sussex, then this is not like that.

Armed with nothing more than a breakfast baguette from the not very posh Posh Nosh XPress burger van and an intentionally light wallet (I have a melon baller, I don't need any more crap), I begin the Journey into What People Are Trying to Get Rid Of. This could also be known as the Journey into What People Really, Really Wanted Five Years Ago.

Beside the very first car, an eight-year-old girl with an evidently minuscule attention span is standing dressed in a diamanté playsuit with tiara and tan, amid the detritus of her childhood. Pre-loved plastic games, dolls, figurines, cuddly toys and more cuddly toys and many more cuddly toys form a frankly shocking toy mountain, enough to indebt the most affluent of families. About a quarter of everything in these fields is a plastic toy – tanks with missing missiles, games with missing counters, Nerf guns with missing Nerfs, dolls with missing limbs. I count seven Buzz Lightyears, all abandoned. This is the real *Toy Story* and there is no happy ending.

It's not just the kids though. Grown-ups are equally bad. Abandoned hobbies account for at least another quarter of items for sale: golf clubs (hundreds), tennis rackets (tens), boxing gloves, punch bags, ice skates, many treadmills, many more fishing rods, a full-size poker table. The pace of technology takes no prisoners either: every other stall has a Game Boy, a PlayStation 1 or 2, a Lean, Mean Fat Grilling Machine, a VHS recorder, a fax machine, a DVD player or a bread machine. So many bread machines. And Maxell audio tapes. And nasal hair trimmers. And bags of mice (the clickable kind). And Morphy Richards Professional Thermoceramic Stylers (okay, just one of them).

How fickle is our taste in entertainment. Books, CDs and DVDs all hint at long-over crazes. The *Friends* box set, the *Friends* mug tree, the *Friends* board game, the *Deal or No Deal* board game, *Lost* Series One, Dan Brown, Dan Brown, Dan Brown, Harry Potter, Dan Brown, *Bananarama* by Bananarama, *All By Myself* featuring Simply Red, Wet Wet Wet, Billy Ocean, Living in a Box and much, much more. *My Life, My Way*, Cliff Richard's putdownable autobiography, *Learning to Fly* by Victoria Beckham, and David

Hasselhoff's *Making Waves,** the warts and all account of a life being the Hoff.

'Look, mate, I gave £9 for it,' says a man selling the motor for a garden strimmer. 'There's no point in me selling it for £11.'

'I'll give you £11.50.'

'No, it's £15.'

'I'll give you £12.'

'No, it's £15.'

'Final offer, £12.50.'

'Jesus, mate. Are you deaf?'

'I'm walking away.'

'Okay, £13. Deal or no deal?'

With the few pounds I had dared to bring, I remain conservative. I haven't got the bartering skills to get properly engaged. So I buy only a definitive book of body language ('stop being so defensive'), a complete set of Manchester United magazines, a life-size polystyrene tiger, a plinth, a 1:146 scale model of HMS *Victory*, a three-in-one rechargeable portable jump-starter (12V with air compressor) and a go-kart which cost the man ninety when

---

* First line, just in the extremely unlikely case you don't have Knight Rider's autobiography on your bookshelf: 'The stage manager asked me, "Are you all right?"' which is better than, 'It was a dark and stormy night,' but not quite the best opening line to a book ever which is, of course: 'Many years later, as he faced the firing squad, Colonel Aureliano Buendía was to remember that distant afternoon when his father took him to discover ice.'

he bought it for his grandchildren and 'They loved it but the tyre has gone and you'll need to get a new bolt on the brake and it needs a bit of a clean-up and I'm asking fifteen but you can take it off me hands for nine.'

'Seven?'

'Nine.'

'Eight?'

'Nine.'

'Nine?'

'Nine.'

We could end this chapter by drawing the positives, couldn't we? Despite the rampant, credit-card-torturing, wet-lipped, fat-bottomed frenzy we get ourselves into, not just ONLINE ON CHRISTMAS DAY but all the other days we can spend, spend, spend, especially when there's a bargain to be had, even if it means ditching all English reserve and trampling fellow shoppers like you're a bull and this is a Pamplonan china shop, there are plus points. The ancient relationship between monger and mongee is being rekindled. No, not kindled. Stop being so digital. *Rekindled*. Your Tesco and your Amazon aren't killing the high street, they're just maiming it a bit. And, to stretch the metaphor, the high street is coming back with lots of physiotherapy and bionic limbs, limbs that offer, umm, quality products, the sort of foodstuffs we can show off about at our pretentious dinner parties. We are in the age of independent shops and farmers' markets. Independent websites and online farmers' collectives aren't doing badly either. And the modern shopping centre isn't as hellish as it used to be even ten years ago. There's glass and light and breathable air . . . and some of them have Wagamamas. And a bowl of kare loman at Wagagmamas, in all its pseudo-Asian, chain-restaurant glory, is as close to heaven as you can get in a shopping centre, which is surprisingly close. You could even argue that the boot fair plastic mountain at the arse end of this whole materialist orgy is actually very, very eco. It's proper, close-circuit recycling after all.

And yet.

We would all be happier if we bought less crap. If we didn't have acute iLust. If we didn't yearn for the latest tablet, phone, console or, if this list is getting too blokey, handbag. Don't say you don't. Yes, you do.

You do.

Do and no returns.

Three months on, the as-it-turns-out-unrepairable go-kart has gone to the dump. From there it will either be shipped to China to be made into drinks cans, plastic bags or, if the reincarnation machine is feeling particularly sym-metrical, a new go-kart. Or it will be flogged on the side to a bric-a-brac man who will sell it for £8 at the next car boot. Repeat ad infinitum.

And I fixed the football table, by the way. It's in the falling-down shed. We use it for keeping the garden-chair cushions off the ground.

THE SPORTS FIELD

He dribbles a lot and the opposition don't like it –
you can see it all over their faces.

RON ATKINSON, Ronglishman

EVERYTHING CHANGED IN 2012. We started it all English. Plucky losers. We finished it all Australian. Cocky winners. Better than Australian even. Australian without the rising inflection at the end of every sent^ence. And some months after the candles were blown out on the London Games and everyone across the land had decided that now, magically or perhaps by osmosis, we were a sporting nation, I find myself standing in lane two of the Sheffield Athletics Arena 100-metre track.

In lane three, Deo Milandu, a nineteen-year-old dec-athlete aiming for Rio, is pacing angrily. In lane four, Liam Ramsay, nineteen-year-old England Athletics U20 Indoor Heptathlon champion, is stretching threateningly. Both are capable of sub-eleven-second hundreds although both are also nursing injuries. I am not nursing an injury. I'm just nursing physical decline. My personal best, two decades ago, before alcohol and lard ruined my otherwise perfect body, was 15.4 seconds.

It had seemed like a good idea at the time. In the post-Olympic glow, a healthier version of the post-coital IKEA hot dog, I had phoned City of Sheffield Athletics, the club that made Jessica Ennis.

'Hello,' I had said. 'I've been inspired by the Olympics.'

'Yes, it has inspired a generation,' agreed the Yorkshireman on the other end of the line. Or words to that effect.

'Can I come up for a trial?'

'Umm.'

When I arrive at the remarkably swish indoor athletics track, I am greeted by Mike Corden, president of the club, and Shaun Hird, the coaching coordinator. Both were national-level athletes in their day: Mike was a Team GB decathlete at Montreal, Shaun was a top middle-distance runner. Now they run one of the most successful clubs in the country. You would expect them to be hopping, skipping and jumping around with post-Games excitement.

'It was a good show,' says Mike, friendly but less hop-skip-jumpy than I'd expected. 'It's a fantastic way to introduce sport to a wider audience. It's entertainment.'

'Hasn't it inspired a generation?' I ask. 'I definitely read that it had inspired a generation. Aren't we all going to become Australian now?'

They both snort, not in an entirely derisive way, but they clearly haven't bought into that particular slogan. Shaun says they've had hundreds of people coming down to the club in the weeks and months since the Games which is great but they don't have the staff or the resources. 'Below the elite level, the level focused on winning medals for a very small group of top athletes, there is no money,' adds Mike.

Shaun and Mike don't get paid to work at their club. They give up forty hours a week of their time as volunteers to coach athletes who might one day be going for gold. The athletes themselves must also make huge sacrifices. Many are forced to live on the dole, the only way they can create enough time to train. If they are injured, there's no money for treatment. If they need transport, they have to thumb a lift. It's a long way from the moneyed world of football.

'Inspiring a generation is like inspiring someone to drive a Formula One car or swim the Channel,' says Mike. 'Without training, I'd die on the first corner or I'd drown halfway across. Or less than halfway across. Without a proper system in place, without training, the inspiration is pointless.'

'But. But. But. Surely if we're all up for it, that's a start?'

'Are we really up for it? Time has eroded the school sports curriculum. Less kids run cross-country. Less kids play football. Lots of schools have amazing facilities but there's no self-motivation among the kids. We've got to get back to proper physical education. We've got to get fit.'

'Well, look, I've come all this way. Can I have a go at the hundred anyway?'

'We can do better than that,' says Mike. 'See those two lads there. Both all-schools champions. You can race with them.'

And so here I am in lane two. The starting pistol fires. Liam and Deo go on the 'b' of bang. I go some time after the 'ang'. Keep your head down for as long as possible, said a friend who likes to think he's sporty. Thirty. Forty. Going well. They're not that far in front. Well, they are but it's not completely embarrassing. Fifty. Sixty. Getting a little tired now. Still in it. Seventy. They've finished. I'm finished, but not in a good way. My head starts to wag, my arms start to flail, the shape has gone. From the mists of time, I hear Mr Ebbage, my old PE teacher, yelling at me to 'get a blimming move on, Rudd.' Ninety. Ninety-five. I'm going to need to have a lie-down. Ninety-eight. Christ, where is the line? Dip for the finish. Dip further to stop my lungs popping out.

'Well done, mate,' says Liam, the patronising little so-and-so with his 10.96 seconds.

'Very good,' says Deo, with his 11.2.

There is no need to record my time. As we've established, it isn't the point. Shaun congratulates me anyway. 'Not bad with no training, no warming up, no spikes, no . . .'

'Really? What do I need to do to improve?'

'You need to relax your shoulders, drive your elbows, develop a tall posture, get your heels up under your but-tocks, get your knees up and your toes up, you need to land on the ball of your foot and drive down and back. Correct all that and you will improve your time. But you won't be going to Rio.'

THE ENGLISH ARE as good as anyone at deciding to become more sporty. It's the actual becoming sporty we find tricky. The average gym membership lasts eighteen months but the average gym attendance lasts much less. It follows a set pattern: initial exuberance, usually in January, followed by gradual decline (to an average of 0.9 visits per week), followed by a few months of non-attendance followed by the final acceptance that the dream is over. And with a lazy click, the direct debit is cancelled. And yet, despite this faltering approach to personal fitness, there is also a strangely optimistic relationship with sport.

We invented a lot of sports and we still expect to do terribly well in them. It isn't realistic. There are 193 other countries in the world and most of them have better hand–eye coordination than us. Football, cricket, rugby, conkers . . . ours, all ours, then embraced by other countries, then used to thrash us with soundly. Even tiddlywinks, a fine sport patented by Londoner Joseph Assheton Fincher in 1888, is now lost to the Americans. And yet we still expect. Or we like to pretend to expect.

There is still one sport at which we will always be undisputed kings. This sport may require very little skill, agility or strength but it demands immense stamina, patience, determination and, above all, manners. Today, on an inhospitably showery summer morning, on the beautifully manicured lawns of Wimbledon, I am lucky enough to be standing face to face with one of the true greats of the sport. John Barnett, a retired design engineer from Tenbury Wells in Worcestershire, doesn't look like a professional sportsman but here he is, right at the front of the race, showing very few signs of fatigue.

'How are you feeling, John?'

'I'm fine, thanks,' he replies.

'And how do you rate your chances?'

'Well, it's a game of two halves. We've got everything to play for as long as we play our game, not their game.'

John is a world-champion queuer – and right now he's in the mother of all queues. He's in the queue for Centre Court tickets. He has been queuing with his daughter Charlotte in car park ten outside the All England Lawn Tennis Club for fourteen hours already. He arrived yesterday evening and took his place at number 510 in the queue for today's tickets. Even though this puts him quite near the front – there are already 7,000 people behind him – it doesn't sound like world-class queuing. But he's not here for today's tennis. He's here for tomorrow. He has another twenty-nine hours to go before he sees his first serve.

'Are you mad?' I ask, jogging on the spot to keep warm.

'No, you have to queue for today's play because the stewards don't start issuing queue tickets for tomorrow until later this morning,' he explains, hardly a bead of sweat on him. 'About an hour ago, they asked those of us here for to-morrow's play to wait over by the fence. Then they moved us here with our tents. We'll get our queue tickets for to-morrow's play later.'

When this happens, John and Charlotte will be in third and fourth place. Bronze medal contention.

'It is wonderfully well organised,' says John. 'A girl has already been along checking how many people we have in each tent so there can be no cheating.'

It is true, it is wonderfully well organised. Stewards resplendent in panama hats and hi-vis jackets are ensuring every last bit of queue etiquette is adhered to and in case anyone is unsure what that might entail, they're also handing out twenty-five-page booklets entitled, 'A Guide to Queuing'. Across the centre pages, nine key rules are enshrined in the Queue Code of Conduct.

Number one states the obvious: 'You are in The Queue if you join it at the end and remain in it until you have acquired a ticket at the turnstiles.' Two to nine ensure there can be no room for rule-bending. You cannot, for instance, reserve a place in The Queue for somebody else, other than in their short-term absence (e.g. toilet break, purchase of refreshments, etc.). Two-person tents, maximum (none of your Mongolian yurts). No barbecues (this is not a festival). No gazebos. Pizza deliveries must be arranged at the Wimbledon Park Road gate only. And it's only one bottle of wine per person. Above all, QUEUE JUMPING WILL NOT BE TOLERATED, it shouts in caps.

'This is actually not such a long queue,' says John, who has been competing for fourteen years. 'Once, there were 30,000-odd. They let about 20,000 in so those 10,000 extra were just queuing in the hope that others would leave. Sometimes you see people still queuing at 7 p.m.'

'You're saying that as though they're the crazy ones but you're the guy sitting in his tent for three days to watch a bit of tennis.'

'I know. We do put ourselves out but we're guaranteed to get what we want. If we didn't put in the hours, we might not get in. And besides, it's a great atmosphere.'

'You enjoy queuing?'

'We see other queuers here year after year. There's one lady who always camps. She's eighty-five years old.'

'Are you not tempted to flog your golden place in the queue to a lazier, richer tennis fan?'

'You just can't. Say I'm number 143 in the queue. The person who is number 144 has been standing behind me for twenty-four hours. What the hell are they going to say if I suddenly vanish and some complete stranger takes my place? Anyway, the rules clearly stipulate you cannot sell your place.'

'Right, but have you ever seen any queue-jumping?'

There is silence. John exchanges a dark look with his daughter. He looks at his feet. She fiddles with the guy ropes. It's just like the time we found out Ben Johnson's magic world record was a little bit too magic.

'We have seen it,' he says eventually. 'But on the whole, it's dignified. It's brilliant.'

'Well, best of luck.'

'Thank you.'

'IT'S QUITE SERIOUS. It's quite competitive. You're not going to be able to chat a lot. You're not going to be able to take notes. Maybe you should just watch? Are you sure you want to play? Really? I mean, you don't have to, I mean, it's not much fun anyway.'

'Okay, I won't play.'

'I really don't think you should play.'

'I won't play.'

'I really think it might be best if you just watch.'

'Fine.'

'Fine.'

'Jesus.'

In my attempt to understand the second most important sport in England after queuing, I had asked if I could join a five-a-side football match at Finsbury Leisure Centre for one morning only. It was a social game. Not a league match. There were no medals or trophies or even seventh division points. Nothing counted on the game's outcome, except, perhaps, pride.

'Bring your kit just in case.'

I got there fifteen minutes early, apprehensive, because of that last phrase. I had decided, after much deliberation, not just to bring my kit but to wear it and had been forced to explain myself to Mehmet the Coffee Guy on platform one.

'I might be playing with one of the most competitive teams in London.'

'They will kill you. Have you got shin pads?'

'No.'

'You shouldn't play.'

'I'm almost certainly not going to play.'

'You really shouldn't play.'

'I'm not going to.'

And I really wasn't going to until Jack didn't turn up.

'Where's Jack?' said a swarthy-looking chap doing keep-me-ups by the goal. He had shin pads and everything.

'I don't know,' said everyone else, also bedecked in shin pads.

'So we're a man short,' said the swarthy chap, still doing keepie-uppies. 'Let's start. Have you got a white top?'

He looked at me. They all looked at me. I looked at them. Three of them were quite short. Three of them were not short enough for my liking. Three of them were properly tall. The three short ones were quite old. Noticeably greying. Audibly creaky. No problem. The three who weren't short enough were not old enough as well. Two-thirds of the three properly tall ones were young as well. And mean-looking. And far, far too serious. It's only a game.

I nodded in a casual yet confident way. As if to say, 'Of course I have a white top. I've got lots of different-coloured tops. You would not believe how many tops I've got. You name it, I've got it.'

'What position do you play?'

'Ummmmmmm.'

'Forward?'

'Errrrrrrrr.'

'Midfield?'

'Hmmmmm.'

'Okay, you're in goal.'

I put on the white top and jogged manfully onto the Astroturf, did some stretches and a couple of short sprints as if to say, 'No problem. Goalie is good.' Whereas I was actually thinking, Where the hell is this man called Jack? Why is Jack late? Why could he not, for once in his pathetic, unpunctual life, be on time? Is that so much to ask, Jack? Really, Jack? I hate you, Jack.'

Still, it probably wouldn't be that bad.

'Keep the shape. Keep the shape. Come on, whites. Focus. FOCUS! Keep the shape. Naz. Naz. Naz. Man on. Naz. Anyone fancy it? Man on. Si. Naz. Si. Man on. Naz. John. Si. Man on. Get on him. Get on him. Well played, John. Oh, come on. Lazy defending, boys. Lazy. Shit. Naz. John.'

I was once told by a footballist that while you need natural talent to become a top striker, you can learn to be a good goalie. Perhaps not a Premiership goalie but maybe Championship. Your Bristol City or your Burnley, for example. Goalkeeping is more nurture than nature. It's teachable. And while you might not make the £200,000 a week your fancy forwards get paid at the very top of the top flight, you can still clear £200,000 a year. When I was told this, it seemed like an incredibly viable career option for one or more of my sons. They have been born into an uncertain world with an uncertainer future. Where are the guaranteed jobs? Not banking. The civil service isn't what it was. Obviously not journalism. Maybe keeping goal was the only reliable job for life?

For the last three years, I've been training my eldest son intensively. Morning, noon and night, he stands between the garden chair and a flowerpot and I kick balls at him, the football equivalent of the Williams sisters.

He is now seven and quite promising. In a year or two, Burnley will send a scout to our back garden and he will be amazed. I will then cut a hard deal via an unscrupulous agent and this is how we will pay for my old people's home when I am ninety, pensionless because my pension company frittered it all away, and refusing to die because of unnecessary improvements in medical science.

On the Finsbury Astroturf, it immediately became apparent that my cunning plan had flaws. For a start, I was bored and tense. This is a horrible combination of emotions, and no way for a man to live his professional life. At the other end, players were running around, shouting, enjoying themselves while I just stood there waiting, waiting for my moment to shine or become a laughing stock.

Eventually, a man in a non-white shirt cut past our defence with a beautiful dummy and an unbeautiful blatant foul which, for some reason, people ignore in five-a-side. He had all the space he needed. And all the time. Our eyes met for a second as he wound up to take his shot. He gave me a malevolent look and snarled in slow motion. I snarled in slow motion back, like the lion at the start of an MGM movie. The ball took off two, maybe three feet from the ground, slicing towards me, a perfect half volley and every novice goalie's nightmare. I fell to my knees and time stood still.

In that moment, I saw that no matter how many balls I kick at my eldest son, he will never be a second-rate goalie. It is no way to live. Your week, your season, your life hinges on one moment of luck under intense pressure. It is not a nice pressure. It is the same pressure that led to England goalie Robert Green's fumble in the 2010 World Cup against the USA. All the time that shot was coming to him, in slow motion, a voice in his head must have been saying, 'Just stop the ball, Rob. It's not rocket science. You've done it 10,000 times before. This is what you do, Rob. It's easy . . .' And another, eviler voice must have been saying, 'This is important, Rob. This is the World Cup. A nation's hopes and dreams rest in your gloves. And it's only the USA. And it's not even a hard shot to save, is it? Look at it just trickling towards you. My mum could save that, Rob. Imagine if you fumbled it, and it rolled in. Wow, can you imagine? That would be absolutely awf— oh bum.'

And all I was thinking was, This isn't that important. It's only a meaningless kick-around among friends, Matt. But they're not your friends, Matt. They are strangers and half of them will be absolutely furious if you fumble this save. And they will judge you. You will be judged. And there will be no return from that judgement. In Italy, you are judged by what you wear and how close you can sit next to complete strangers on a beach. In France, you are judged by the quality of your mistress and the strength of your musk. In Sweden, you are judged by the cleanliness of your Thule roof box and the minimalism of your reading glasses. But here, in England, in this moment, I would be judged solely on my ability to save a meaningless goal.

I caught the ball. I rolled ostentatiously onto my side, stood up and bounced it a couple of times like professional goalkeepers do in proper matches to give the impression they are entirely unruffled. Piece of cake. The whites clapped a bit. Someone said, 'Nice save, Matt.'

'Come on!' I yelled too loud, filled with confidence. I would not be the Robert Green of Finsbury Leisure Centre. Everyone looked at me as if to say, 'Calm down, mate. It's only a game.' Then Jack turned up and I was back on the bench.

BRIAN BUCK IS England's most enthusiastic football supporter. He has been to more than 10,000 football matches since his first, Cambridge United versus Colchester United Reserves at the Abbey Stadium, in 1954. He goes to at least one game a day except Sundays when he goes to church, and although he supports Spurs and has missed only one home match at White Hart Lane since 1968, he is happy watching any team at any level from the Premier League right down to the man-and-his-dog kick-about. What is wrong with him?

'I think my real interest started when my father took me to watch Spurs beat Birmingham City 6–0 in 1960, the year they last won the double,' he tells me. 'I'd never been interested in playing or watching the game but the atmosphere that night was overwhelming and I was hooked. I can't really describe how I felt at the time, but for years I replayed that match in my head, kicking every ball with them, to the point where I couldn't sleep at nights. I even made my sister recite the Spurs Double team over breakfast each day.'

He says football was good because you could watch it just as comfortably by yourself or with other people. I don't get this. The same applies to *EastEnders* which is indoors and the seating is more comfortable. Why venture out in the cold, dark months, come rain or shine but mainly, let's be honest, rain, to watch other people, usually overpaid and undereducated, kick a ball around a field?

'It's what I've always done and I don't know any different,' he says. 'I know that I'm a bit eccentric, but I've reached the age where I don't really care what other people think. It's like being a chain smoker or an alcoholic except that I don't want to give it up and I don't have to. I will continue to watch football until the day I die. I love England and my love of the game has taken me to more than 3,000 grounds up and down the country. I see my friends all over the place. It's like a mobile social club.'

There's something very pleasing about Brian's obsessive behaviour. If it was trains rather than football, we'd probably tease him. If it was Angelina Jolie, we'd probably lock him up. But Brian has found his true love (after his wife, of course) and it is the calm contemplation of the beautiful game. He has found his place in life and it just happens to be on a terrace, any terrace, where he is accepted and respected by his fellow football fans. It feels straightforward, simple and, above all, tempting.

'COME ON, SON. Get your stuff. We're going to the football.'

Son, who will no longer be a £200,000-a-year second-rate goalie, is excited. So am I. We have tickets to see Reading play at home. We are going to Reading. Woohoo. Who says woohoo about Reading? In the woohoo league, I put it quite a long way below Miami and Rio de Janeiro and Birmingham and Coventry. I put it just above Croydon. But, on Reading's southern side is the Madejski Stadium, home of Reading Football Club. And Reading Football Club is doing rather well. Promoted to the Premiership last season, it has a perfervid, yet civilised fan base. Perfect.

Our seats are between a man eating very strong sardine sandwiches out of a satchel and another man with a how-does-he-get-through-job-interviews tattoo on his neck.* Behind us sit a mother and daughter, arguing about homework, *Made in Chelsea* and a midfielder's hamstring injury. Two rows in front are two men in almost matching pink shorts and wax jackets with absolutely no tattoos on their necks. It is an eclectic crowd and an eclectic stadium. The main sponsor is Waitrose which, for a game with working-class roots, is not very working class at all.** Will the teams be served hors d'oeuvres rather than sliced orange at half-time?

Practically speaking, it is bitterly cold and the plastic nursery seats are bitterly uncomfortable. My son huddles against me. I huddle against the man with the sardine sandwiches. The man with the neck tattoo has dressed sensibly with several thermal layers which just goes to show you shouldn't judge a book by its cover.†

In spite of the inclement conditions, Son is beside himself with excitement, primarily because a man with an

---

* Maybe a neckerchief?

** Top three favourite I Shop At Waitrose Because . . . backfiring campaign tweets from September 2012: 'I shop at Waitrose because . . . Clarissa's pony just will not eat value straw' (Dear Evie). 'I shop at Waitrose because . . . I once heard a six-year-old boy say, "Daddy, does Lego have a 't' at the end like 'merlot?'"' (Ben Jones). And 'I shop at Waitrose because . . . you say "Ten items or fewer" not "Ten items or less", which is important' (Alistair Coleman).

† I know this because we have a long conversation about the merits of Thinsulate as opposed to Icebreaker.

enormous pneumatic hand-grenade launcher is firing mini-footballs into the crowd, encouraged by Kingsley Lion, a seven-foot bipedal cat masquerading as the team mascot. I wonder if they had the hand-grenade launcher or the cat at the first match that hooked Brian Buck. I wonder if my son will get hooked. Then I wonder if I'd prefer him to become a chain-smoking alcoholic rather than a man who has attended 10,000 football matches. Then the game begins.

Nothing much happens until the end of the first half when one of the opposition – or scum as the people in pink shorts two rows in front call them – falls over. Even at a distance of more than 100 yards, it looks like a dive. Our man was nowhere near him. The referee takes a different view from the 18,000 Reading fans and shows our man, our completely innocent man, our Reading One, the red card. As players surround the ref, we all go mad. Not please-transfer-me-to-the-supervisor mad. Not these-duck-eggs-aren't-up-to-Waitrose's-usual-standard mad. Pure, proper, tear-up-the-seats mob outrage. The insulated, tattooed man is muttering. The man with the sardines has started to pack away his lunchbox. The mother and daughter are screaming the kind of profanities mothers and daughters shouldn't scream individually let alone in unison. Son and I are standing on our plastic potties, yelling and booing and telling the other team they suck. This is what theatre used to be like before the Victorians made it polite. Wild audience participation. The exact opposite of good sportsmanship.

It's incredibly good fun, though of course terrible, shocking and hardly a good example for a six-year-old.

One of the men in the wax jackets takes it further. Even after we have all returned, grumbling, to our seats, he stands, puce with rage. He doesn't sit down for the rest of the afternoon.

At the end of the day, it's a game of two halves and the referee's egregious error is not pivotal. We draw. We all funnel out of the stadium singing songs, arm in arm, united in sport and barely contained tribal brutality.

> *We all follow the Reading,*
> *Over land and sea (and Oxford),*
> *We all follow the Reading,*
> *On to victory. All together now.*

The following Saturday, I take the boys to the garden centre and then we have lunch at Pizza Express.

It isn't the same.

I CAN SEE THE POINT OF FOOTBALL, but I refuse to see the point of golf. Nope. Sorry. Not listening. Fingers in ears. Lalalalala. Mark Twain said it was a good walk spoiled but it's not even a good walk. Golf is a bad walk through a vomit of rhododendron, water features, lurid green grass and sandpits your children are not allowed to play in. Then there are the golfers themselves. A company that specialises in 'energising marketing to golfers in England', tells prospective clients that golfers are an 'affluent audience', a 'financial powerhouse', 'decision-makers'. The golf course is 'where the barriers are down', where these monstrous-sounding people 'go to relax, discuss (and deal), where they have the time to absorb (the speed filters are off) and where they are looking for conversation stimulus (like your brand)'. Bleurgh.

They might be financial powerhouses – well done them – but they certainly aren't relaxed. Golf is a frustrating game played by people who are easily frustrated. It's a fatal combination that makes golf courses snooty and unpleasant places.

Let us glance randomly and not at all selectively at recent golf stories that have been in the news. Ah, here we go. A fifty-four-year-old golfer called Harold attacked another fifty-four-year-old golfer called Barry with his eight iron after accusing him of playing his ball. You won't read about this in the golf-marketing literature but Harold was arrested at the golf course near Luton and charged with assault occasioning actual bodily harm.

'I was knocked to my knees,' Barry told the court. 'I can recollect covering my face to try to ward off the blows.'

The prosecutor opened the case by telling the jury that, 'Although golf is usually thought to be a relaxing pastime, on this day in September it was not.'

Objection, Your Honour. This incident is entirely representative of all golf courses all the time. Golf is not relaxing.

Going for a walk in non-stupid clothes without a bag of metal sticks is relaxing. Snorkelling is relaxing. Watching the Jewellery Channel is relaxing. Golf? Nope.

'Yes it is,' says Mike, my only golfing friend (the others have been got rid of and he will be too once he has fulfilled his usefulness). 'Don't be so prejudiced.'

'Shut up, golfer.'

'You shut up.'

'You shut up.'

'We'll play a round and I bet you take it back.'

'Fine.'

'Fine.'

And at first, one morning in Sussex, Mike was right. It was quite relaxing in a frustrating, why-didn't-we-hire-a-buggy-or-just-go-to-the-pub kind of way. The sun was out. If I focused carefully, I could see unblemished countryside in the distance that hadn't been obliterated by the golf course. But then the people behind us caught up and started watching. And disapproving. And then barging through because they were wearing chequered trousers and we weren't. According to the golf marketing company, these people are 16 per cent more likely to be leaders than me. You could tell.

After this, my bad golfery deteriorated further. I found sand, bushes, water, pavements and, on one forgettable occasion, the outer reaches of an adjacent shopping centre. All the time, more golfists turned up behind us and agitated like we were on a motorway and they were driving Audis. In my mind, I resolved that if one of them attacked me with an eight iron, I would attack back with a five and we'd both sit in the dock at Luton Crown Court/Sussex equivalent.

Then I was nearly killed.

'Fore!' shouted a distant man some time after he hooked his ball woefully off the fairway but only one millisecond before it whistled past my head. I always thought you shouted fore before you played your shot. Not here. Not today. I paused momentarily to recall the recent news of a man who had lost an eye after someone on a different hole mistimed their first shot (another entirely representative golf story). Then I thought how close I had just come to never again seeing my children with both eyes. Then I became quite angry.

'You idiot,' I shouted, walking towards him.

'Get out of the bloody way then,' he shouted back, which was not quite as apologetic as I'd been expecting.

'We're not in the way. We're not even on your fairway.'

'I shouted fore. You're supposed to watch out.'

'You shouted fore about an hour after you'd hit the ball. You should give everyone a little bit more warning if you're that rubbish. Or maybe wait until no one else is around.'

Or slightly swearier words to that effect.

'It must be you,' says my only golfing friend. 'I normally have a lovely time.'

It must be me. In order to give golf another chance/to reinforce my completely understandable prejudice, I ask for a tour of Wentworth, one of the most exclusive clubs in

England. This is the home of Bruce Forsyth, no less. It is in Surrey. In 2007 it made headlines for blackballing a female member after it was revealed, so to speak, that she had once been a Page Three girl. As the *Sun* put it at the time: 'Jealous wives feared the 38DD model might end up playing around – with their hubbies. Furious Liz said yesterday: "It's ridiculous."' More understandably, Premiership footballers have been ejected for wearing denim.

I arrive and already it looks bad: rhododendrons and Range Rovers everywhere; caddies in boiler suits, valets, concierges, greensmen cutting fairways with nail scissors, three old duffers having lunch at their usual table; Clegg hammer tests on the greens; swans. It costs £15,000 a year to be a full member here, plus the £7,000 joining fee. Non-members pay almost £300 a round.

'It's a sport for rich people with a lot of time,' says my guide when I ask where all the young people are. 'Rich young people don't have a lot of time.'

This is exactly the sort of place where people who have made a lot of cash shuffling money that isn't theirs from one hedge fund to another like to hang out with their own, I conclude as I peruse the lunch menu. Still, the boudin of foie gras with black cherry compote and toasted brioche sounds good for £15 and, if I were one of those hedge-funders, I wouldn't say no to the Sussex Downs lamb with crispy sweetbreads, summer vegetables and girolles for £28 to follow. Or indeed the Wentworth sticky toffee pudding with caramel ice cream to finish.

And then I might have a bit of a rub down in the spa.

And a swim.

And a splash of Glenlivet to ease the stock market jangles a little later.

No, right. I'm not here for that. I'm here to show golfism for what it really is. And right on cue, I spot a man in his sixties having the arms taken in on a green blazer while his wife looks on. This is not sport. He won't even play golf in the blazer. He'll wear it in the clubhouse for a conversation about futures derivatives (if those are things) while the wife sits at home choosing fabrics for new curtains she doesn't need.

'Hello,' I say, expecting him to go puce-faced at my temerity.

'Hello,' he replies warmly.

'Hello,' adds the wife.

'What's the point of golf?' I ask, not fooled.

'It's the challenge,' he says.

'It's like a crossword puzzle with a lovely view,' adds the wife.

'You both play?'

'Yes, we do,' says the wife.

'A lot of men here would love it if their wives played. I'm Alan, by the way. This is Val.'

'It's not really a proper sport though, is it? It's all about the green blazers.' I'm not being fooled by their pretend niceness. 'It's all about the club.'

'Well, if you're asking if I'd rather be here than in the office, then yes, it is very nice here. We're lucky really.'

'Yes, but answer the question. It's not like football, is it?'

'We had our second date at a football match,' says Val. 'Alan took me to see Chelsea versus Man United.'

'At the Shed,' says Alan, looking into the middle distance nostalgically. 'Very romantic. You're right though. Golf is different.'

I'm not getting anywhere with these two. They're doing a very convincing job of being happy, reasonable people. Not puce-faced at all. I storm off, puce-faced, ignoring the smiling doorman and the chap chasing after me with my bag. A swan says something derogatory as I drive past its pond.

Exactly.

SATURDAY AFTERNOON AT THE Vine cricket ground, Sevenoaks, Kent, the oldest cricket ground in the world.* I'm sitting on a bench with a German called Alice and we're waiting for the opening batsmen to arrive.

'So you hit the ball through the sticks and another man chases you?' she says, like she's grappling with a completely ridiculous concept.

---

* Like all oldest things, this is disputed. Henfield (1777) and Chalvington and Ripe (1762) have claimed to be the oldest but the first recorded game at the Vine took place on 6 September 1734. Mitcham Cricket Club in Surrey claims it has been up and running since 1685 but evidence is sketchy and I live nearer the Vine so it will do.

'No, no, no, no, no, Alice. You have to hit the sticks with a ball and the other man tries to hit the ball with the bat. And then he runs between the sticks while the other man runs the other way.'

'And there are hoops?'

'No.'

'And you swing the bit between his legs?'

'No.'

'And it's not really running?'

'Croquet. You're thinking of croquet. Cricket is like, umm, baseball. You know baseball?'

'Of course.'

'Well, cricket is like that but with LBWs, creases, cutters, beamers, grubbers, zooters, yorkers, mullygrubbers, peaches, cherries, ducks, golden ducks, platinum ducks, in-swingers, out-swingers, silly mid-offs, silly mid-ons, silly nannies, leg breaks, leg byes, leg slips, leg cutters, legs before wickets, gullies, dilscoops, googlies, hoodoos, wafts, wags, chin music, Mr Xavier Tras and, of course, luncheon.'*

One bench along, four old duffers slip in and out of contented consciousness. Two of them have brought their own deluxe garden recliners. Four-packs of John Smith's Extra Smooth are being worked through slowly.

---

* I didn't include gazunder, my favourite cricketing term, which is Australian for a ball that doesn't bounce as high as expected. It gaz under the bat. This would have confused German Alice beyond repair.

'I'm trying to explain cricket to a German,' I tell them as the Vine openers adopt a defensive attitude to Bromley's fast bowlers.

'Have you got six months?' says one.

'No, it's easy,' says another. 'When you're in, you're out and when you're out, you're in.'

'Thanks. Can you tell her why it's so appealing?'

'It's tradition, isn't it?'

'I don't like these metal benches though. What are they? Anti-vandal benches? You need a nice wooden bench if you're going to sit here for seven hours.'

'It's social.'

'It's the next best thing to playing.'

'It's easier to get signed off by your other half than the pub.'

'And look at that lovely view.'

We all look at the lovely view. The bowler shouts, 'Aaaaaaarrrrgggghhhhhhh,' because 'Young-uns never say Howzat any more,' but the umpire is unmoved. We all start tearing up the benches and swearing and packing away sardine sandwiches. Only joking.

'What do you call a German bowler who gets three wickets with three balls?' asks the third old duffer when Alice gets bored and goes off shopping. I brace for inappropriateness.

'A jerry-atric.'

I return to my bench, leaving the four of them chuckling.

'Don't tell anyone you saw us nodding off,' shouts one of them, by way of goodbye. And this is exactly what is great about English sport. It isn't winning Olympic medals or European cups or even the Sunday league, although it is terribly important that we pretend it is. No, it is telling bad jokes, cheering a little bit, tutting a lot and then nodding off to the soporific sound of leather on willow or ITV commentary or anything at all to do with golf. It's not the winning or the taking part. It's the merely having something to do on the weekend that isn't shopping or the *X Factor*. Sport, for all the moaning, is our saving grace.

9

THE MOTORWAY

*I don't run a car, have never run a car. I could say that this
is because I have this extremely tender environmentalist
conscience, but the fact is I hate driving.*

DAVID ATTENBOROUGH, on the buses

AUGUST 1983. Third week of the school holidays – and
with only minimal shouting and one U-turn ('Did you turn
off the boiler?' 'No, you said you were going to.' 'Did I?'),
okay two U-turns ('Have you got the address?' 'Where did
you last leave it?' 'Me?'), we were off to North Wales for
a fortnight. On paper, it won't sound good. It would take
many, many hours to get there. When we arrived, it would
be raining. Sideways. We would have to walk the last mile
up the hill to the cottage with all the luggage because the
hill was Mount Snowdon. And the cottage would have
no heating. And North Wales is not, by any stretch of the
imagination, the south of France.

It didn't matter. It was the best holiday ever because we were driving there in a Datsun Cherry. It was no ordinary Datsun Cherry. It was brand-new, an 'A-reg' if you can believe it, replacing the beat-up old Hillman that had only survived so long because Dad's cousin knew a bit about cars.

The Cherry smelled of factory chemicals and Japanese *vorsprung durch technik*. It had a cassette player built in and everything. For context, Dad had sideburns and the tennis rackets at Wimbledon were still wooden. Chicken McNuggets had not been invented. Cheryl Cole was eight weeks old. J.R. Ewing had only just been shot. A Datsun Cherry was the future.

Of course, there were drawbacks. The Cherry had a very small boot so my sister and I had been selflessly volunteered to have most of the luggage – sheets, duvets, wellingtons, groceries, coats, more coats, fishing nets, Monopoly and an easel and seven dolls and my Action Man and a picnic table and a kitchen sink – on our laps. It was very hot. The Cherry had two fans but you wouldn't write home about them. And Mum was afraid of overtaking lorries so we never really got up enough speed to get a through draught.

It didn't matter. We had games. Not PSPs or Apps or Nintendo DSs. Much more exciting games like I Spy, Hangman, Pig, Guess the Make of the Car Overtaking Us and Count Fifty Red Vans Before Northampton.

It still didn't matter. We had stops at motorway service stations and motorway service stations were the most exciting thing in the entire world, even more exciting than a new Datsun Cherry.

On this particular journey, as far as collective family memory can piece together, we stopped four times: once for the toilet (possibly on the M25 but possibly not because it wasn't entirely finished in 1983); once for sandwiches at Newport Pagnell (the sandwiches were homemade which was obviously very disappointing because we could have got trays and gone to the cafeteria and eaten pies on laminate tables but there was a sky bridge which meant I could play Jump the Trucks, another hit in the Rudd Family games compendium); another toilet stop somewhere Leicestershirish; and a Little Chef on an A-road maybe in Shropshire. The anticipation of each stop, the sense of progress, of speed, of being part of the very modern world, of sitting in a Little Chef booth. It seems such a long time ago now. Everything has changed. And nothing.

Do people fall out of love with service stations at a certain age? I was wondering last week at Colsterworth services on the A1 near Grimsthorpe as I ordered a Whopper with Cheese Meal from a boy with more spots than skin but, on the plus side, his whole life ahead of him in all its finite glory. Is there a certain moment in your early twenties, after a period of teenage ambivalence, when the excitement finally gasps its last and all that is left are damp tables, the strong smell of cut-price detergent, the nagging irritation that the spotty boy is so much younger than me, the dispiriting sound of bass-less, baseless musac and the even naggier irritation that everything in this place is insultingly overpriced?

Do children of the twenty-first century have any love for motorway service stations at all? Mine certainly seem less excited than I remember being at their age. Is that because service stations today are synonymous with pausing DVDs 'just at the good bit, Daaaaaaaaad,' and then being banned from the weak-gripped-robot-hand-soft-toy rip-off arcade game? No, it's not that. Service stations have definitely become less lovable, I decided as I negotiated my way through an ironically hazardous obstacle course of wet-floor warning signs on my way to a toilet full of puddles, erectile dysfunction adverts and the most exotic condom machine in the country.*

No. Let's not be rash. Colsterworth might have been having a bad day. Let's do this properly. Let's spend twenty-four hours at Newport Pagnell, not just the first ever motorway service station open to cars, not just one of the very few service stations in the country to receive five stars for its toilets but also home to some of my happiest childhood memories.** Let us analyse the English on

---

* The machine didn't just sell condoms (1 x natural, 1 x dots & ribs, 1 x ultra thin). Oh no, good motorway commuters. It sold Blue Zeus for Men ('enliven and maintain sexual vigour and vitality – herbal supplement') and stimulator rings ('providing the ultimate sexual buzz for him *and* her; battery length up to forty minutes; waterproof').

** I'm exaggerating for the sake of dramatic tension.

the move or at least taking a break from being on the move or at the very least taking a break from being stuck in a traffic jam that should have been on the move. This is us being free, after all. Free from the home and work. Just us and the open road, the nine-lane highway, the Californian sun kissing our cheeks as we drive our Caddy down Route 66. Sorry. Wrong movie. We don't need those clichés. The English open road is a lot less open than the Hollywood one. It has Cone Hotlines and Roadworks Until Spring 2019 and Sorry For the Inconvenience. But it is still the start of all good adventures. And the motorway service station is still a crossroads for all adventurers. Just like Everest base camp, only lower and with worse, more expensive food. Join me in Newport Pagnell. You don't want to join me? Fine, I'll go alone.

I check into the motel not long after lunch and go to my room on the first floor which offers en suite facilities, a tiny kettle, a thousand tiny sachets of sugar, milk and tea and a loud humming noise as standard.

'There's a loud humming noise in my room,' I say to the receptionist.

'I know,' she says. 'It's the boiler.'

'Right.'

'Yes.'

'Umm.'

'It usually goes off in the middle of the night and comes on again at about five.'

'Okay, thanks.'

'Anything else I could help with today, sir?'

'Could I move rooms? I'm not good with loud humming noises.'

Tap tap tap tap. Oh, bum. Tap, tap. Here we go. The computer. Tap tap tap tap. Tap tap. Tap tap. Yes.

'You can upgrade to an executive room for £10 more.'

'I'll take it.'

The deal includes a Hypnos bed, whatever that is, and an executive breakfast instead of the humming noise which is a total bargain. We shake hands on it. I move my stuff. I spend forty-five minutes opening three hundred of the thousand sachets in an attempt to make a nice cup of tea but succumb to paper cuts and boredom, and go for an afternoon stroll around the lorry park instead.

I won't lie to you. Very little is happening in the lorry park. Some lorries are parked. Others aren't. I go to Waitrose and buy a yum-yum instead. Since Waitrose and M&S have started peddling their crayfish-and-rocket-and-iced-pastry-based wares on the hard shoulders of motorways, the English road trip has improved considerably. The Ginster steak pie ('29% beef') and a very long Snickers are no longer the core elements of your road-trip dinner. But still, my Newport Pagnell minibreak is dragging a bit.

For a good thirty minutes – while a young couple have an absolutely jaw-dropping argument about why he always pays for the cinema tickets and she pays for fack all – I consider leaving and making up this next section. Then I go back to the receptionist at the motel to ask the question I have always wanted to ask a motorway-service-station motel receptionist.

'So is this whole thing about people meeting in service stations to have affairs a myth?' I ask.

She looks at me. I look at her. She's going to go all officious and say yes.

'Not at all,' she says, not batting an eyelid. 'We get several a week.'

'Really?'

'Really.'

'How do you know they're not married?'

'You just know. And some of them ask to pay by the hour.'

'Can you pay by the hour?'

'No.'

'That would be a bit seedy.'

'Some of them come in separately. The man first, then the woman.'

'Really?'

'Really.'

We are interrupted by a man checking in separately. He looks at us. We both look at him. Crumpled suit, receding hairline, Vauxhall Vectra key fob, wheelie suitcase (probably empty), almost certainly a total familiarity with novelty motorway-service-station condom machines. Did he kiss his wife goodbye this morning? Did he tell his boss at his IT systems installation firm that he had a meeting with a client in Milton Keynes this afternoon? Is he really here for his fortnightly 'blue-sky meeting' with Tracy from accounts?

According to a survey of actual people, one in six of us think motorway service stations are good (as opposed to soul-destroyingly horrific) places to have a fling. One in twenty of us (claim to) have actually done it. Intriguingly, drivers from the Midlands and the north-west are most prone to the temptations of motel sex as are those aged between thirty-six and forty-five. This man, this forty-three-year-old man with his Midlands accent, his extra splash of aftershave, his loose-fitting wedding ring, is one of them. He scuttles off to his room to prepare the handcuffs, the blindfold and the feather duster. Filthy man. I loiter, investigatively, for the pencil-skirted, home-wrecking harlot who will sneak in a few minutes later, probably in big sunglasses. She doesn't. Maybe there's a back entrance. Maybe she was in the wheelie.

The afternoon passes into evening. Sugar-crazed school trippers, blue-toothed businessmen, Twilight Zone truckers, the dispossessed youth and several chaotic, barely managing young families spill in and out. It has the transience of an airport but not the glamour. Except of course for the loos, a highlight of my Buckinghamshire minibreak.

In 2008 Newport Pagnell North Services was awarded the very highest accolade at the Loo of the Year awards, the Oscars of toilets. What does it take to achieve this honour? What does a five-star toilet look like? Will the seats be lined with the freshly harvested neck fur of alpacas? Will the toilet paper be hand-sewn from the happy tears of baby voles? Will there be handmade soaps, lemon-scented towels, a string quartet, free neck rubs?

None of the above. It is just like all motorway service station toilets but cleaner.

Over canapés, okay peanuts, in the bar of the motel, I express scepticism at the role of Newport Pagnell as impromptu haven of illicit affairs to the Portuguese bartender.

'No, it's really true,' he replies but I should have come later in the week. Wednesdays and Thursdays are peak days for pokery. Mondays are troughs.

'But why don't they go somewhere a bit more, well, romantic?'

'I don't know. Too expensive?' he offered. There is a recession.

'Or maybe it's convenience. You don't want to waste time getting into a city centre hotel?'

Is it just sex with these people? No conversation? No dinner and a movie? At one in the morning, unable to sleep despite the lack of a loud humming noise, I go for a stroll across the car park, through the empty shops and up onto the sky bridge. This must have been the spot I had played Jump the Trucks almost thirty years earlier. The trucks are still flying by, a Sisyphean procession up the backbone of England. Where are they all going? Why? Who cares? I look both ways, checking the coast is clear and I have another jump. And another. Two trucks in one go. Double points. I win. Then I notice two teenagers at the far end of the sky bridge giggling at the middle-aged man clearly having a breakdown. I traipse back to my room and try not to think about all the married people who have spanked differently married people in this very bed.

In the morning, I eat executive congealed baked beans and executive congealed scrambled egg and toast which is deep-fried to prevent congealing. Then I press my trousers, have a coffee, write a postcard and leave three hours earlier than I'd planned. Unless you're having an affair or you are a child in an age before Nintendo, motorway service stations are not very exciting.

THE FIRST STRETCH of what would become the M6 was opened by Harold Macmillan on 5 December 1958 (and promptly closed again for repairs a month later after it froze). It was designed to bypass Preston, not because Preston needed bypassing but because faster cars were no longer compatible with horse-drawn carts. It was carnage on Preston high street. In those early days when everything was black and white and no one had heard of CDs or pasta or MacBook Pros, motorways were the future. They promised freedom and joy where only traffic jams, petrol fumes and horse poo had existed before.

When the first fifty-five-mile stretch of the M1 opened in 1959 connecting the cosmopolitan epicentres of Watford and Rugby,* people queued to get on it. It was busiest on Sundays when families would ride it just to say they had. Not that it was ever that busy, not by today's standards. I've seen the newsreels: Ford Anglias taking it in turns to put-put up the three-lane superhighway, their occupants smiling and laughing at the sheer thrill of doing crazy speeds like 55mph or even more. Until their engines blew up, of course. The AA was up to its ears in those early days. Cars were not designed for motorways. Bits fell off. Pistons melted. But it didn't stop the rictus grinning. England was on the move.

Then came the first motorway service stations. England was on the move but with pit stops.

Then we just got carried away. To hell with trains, let's build lots and lots more motorways.

Then came today. A Friday on the M25. It's not even three in the afternoon, nowhere near rush hour, and already the traffic is slowing down. Today, we have 2,211 miles of motorway and most of it is saturated. The engineers who built the M1 envisaged that it would carry 20,000 cars a day. Today, it does seven times that and counting. At the current rate of congestion, the Department for Transport estimates we will be wasting more than £20 billion of productivity a year sitting in traffic jams by 2025.

---

* No, I'm not being sarcastic. Rugby is the home of rugby, the jet engine and a particularly average Premier Inn. Watford is . . . umm. Watford is . . . umm. Hang on. Watford is the head office for Wetherspoons.

At least I was moving. Sixty miles per hour in the out-side lane – Ford Anglia break-up speed. I had Lana del Rey moaning away only because she'd been left in the CD player by *someone else*, not because I chose her. It's not an openly annoying album in the sense of a Bieber or a Deep Forest but in retrospect I can see that it's the sort of gnaw-ing, sentimental self-indulgence of youth that might be subliminally conducive to angry driving in the middle-aged. Get over yourself, Lana. Like the spotty kid at Burger King, you've got the rest of your life ahead of you and I imagine very little of it will involve slow-moving traffic between Junctions 6 and 7 of the M25. (I haven't, by the way, managed to find any evidence of people getting excited about the M25 when it first opened. My father-in-law remembers jogging on it before it opened but even that wasn't much fun.*)

I was about one and a half chevrons behind the car in front. This is a guess because there weren't any chevrons marked. If there had been, it might have made the Silver Audi Man one-sixteenth of a chevron behind me back off.

I am a law-abiding citizen, more so when others are not abiding by it. I understand that chevrons should be abided by even when chevrons are not there. I under-stand that tailgating doesn't get you there any faster. And

---

* Although, of course, the Brighton & Hove Bus Company is now offering tours of the London Orbital. One whole loop in four hours. The first excursion was fully booked but I'm hoping that might have tailed off a bit by now.

this Audi driver, this sales rep on his way to show yet another disinterested party some misleading brochures on PVC windows or printer cartridges or the benefits of solar panelling, this cock . . . Well, chevrons mean nothing to this sort of person.

As we continued, I felt the pressure getting to me. I had a nice bit of space in front of me, just enough so that I didn't have to slam on the brakes every time the traffic slowed but I could see the silver bell-end in my rear-view mirror, weaving around to demonstrate impatience. His podgy face could not understand why I didn't move over, given the chasm (ten metres) of space in front of me.

I wasn't going to move over. For a start, there was nowhere to move. The middle lane was full and a sign had flashed up suggesting, quite strongly, that we stay in lane.

He weaved some more.

I tested my brake lights by tapping the pedal. They worked. He backed off and mouthed many profanities. But then, like the silver penis he was, he returned for more, tickling my bumper.

He hated me.

And now I hated him.

Then it all kicked off. A Vauxhall Insignia in the middle lane moved into my one and a half chevrons. This annoyed me but it incensed Audi Cock because it confirmed what he suspected: that I was leaving far too much space in front of me. He swung into lane two, zoomed past me and the Vauxhall and then indicated to move back into lane three.

Insignia Guy was not going to let Audi Cock in. He moved forward to within one one-hundred-and-twenty-eighth of a chevron of the car in front. Cock. The first cock, now stuck behind a truck in the middle lane, slowed down and indicated to move in between the second cock and me.

No. Goddam. Way.

With a mirthless cackle, I accelerated to leave one thousandth of a chevron between me and the second cock. In my peripheral vision, I could see Cock A was purple and veiny with rage. For a split second, this gave me more pleasure than the unexpectedly successful birth of my first son after forty-seven hours of relentless, doom-filled labour in which I had nothing to do but pace the many and various rooms we were in, worry about the incessant beeping of hypochondriac monitors and try to tell my beloved it would be all right. Then I noticed Cock B looking at me in his rear-view mirror and had a terrible moment of clarity: I was Cock C. Then we all ground to a halt because three junctions ahead, a butterfly had flapped its wings.

This wouldn't happen if we were ants. According to Tom Vanderbilt, the American author of *Traffic: Why We Drive the Way We Do*, the new world army ant might just be the best commuter in the world. Each morning, after a quick espresso and a fifteen-minute blast of the *Today* programme, millions of them head out from the nest. Those that find food turn back into the oncoming traffic. They don't indicate. They don't wait for the next junction. They just do a

U-turn on the spot. It should be gridlock but it isn't. The ants create a three-lane superhighway. Those heading out from the nest use the outer lanes. Those returning use the middle lane. Despite being almost blind and having an even greater disregard for chevrons than drivers on the M25 the ants manage their daily expeditions to and from work with far greater efficiency than humans.

We mustn't feel bad. Ants have had thousands of years to evolve their supremely efficient motorway-driving style. We've had just over half a century. And ants are all about the community. They're selfless creatures, happy to cooperate for the greater good. We aren't like that, particularly when we get into a car. Particularly if we are male.

WHEN PSYCHOLOGISTS measured stress chemicals in the saliva of people stuck in heavy traffic, they found that men were seven times more stressed than women. They did not do a control study measuring the stress levels of volunteers sitting next to strangers measuring their stress levels but still, the evidence was compelling: men handle stressful driving situations badly. It's to do with the fight-or-flight instinct we've inherited from our hunter-gatherer ancestors.* In a traffic jam, we can neither fight nor fly so we sit there and get stressed.

* So much of the problems with the world are to do with the slow pace of evolution, not least war and nipple rash.

If only we could be more like ants with their all-for-one approach to the motorway. If we all worked together, traffic jams would be a thing of the past. If only there was some kind of supercomputer that could force us all to drive more cooperatively.

'It's called Midas,' says Rob Bell, bronze commander at the South East Regional Control Centre just off Junction 6 of the M25. 'Motorway Incident Detection and Automatic Signalling.'

'Does it have a sexy but non-emotive woman's voice and will it at some point decide humans are no longer worth putting up with and kill us all?'

'No.'

Of course not. Midas is the system that attempts to deal with traffic jams before they happen. A series of loops around the motorway detects slow-moving traffic and triggers lower advisory speeds. When we're hurtling along at eighty and the road is blissfully clear, Midas is the machine telling us to do sixty or forty. It wants us to slow down so that congestion up ahead has time to clear. Not that 'wants' is the right word. It's a computer. It can't want anything but you get the idea.

'These days, it's not just about incident management,' says Rob. 'It's about motorway management. Our primary role is to keep traffic moving.'

The control centre is the size of a basketball court but much cooler. Fifteen desks all face a huge video wall showing various CCTV feeds from the motorways. Each desk has five of its own screens, the main one of which shows a flow diagram of junctions, average speeds and digital signage. Midas runs all this. If she's in the right mood, the operators can manually override her. If I pressed that button, I could bring half of the M25 to a standstill.

'Don't press that button,' says Rob.

'Is Midas the reason we have phantom traffic jams when cars slow down and then start moving again and there's no obvious cause of the delay?' I whisper because Midas might be listening.

'Sometimes, a Midas loop can be triggered by a slow-moving lorry. A guy might miss a gear on a hill and that will automatically trigger a speed limit of forty which would last for fifteen minutes. But most phantom traffic jams are caused by bad driving. When you brake, the guy behind you will brake a bit harder if he's too close. This ripples back to a guy a mile behind who has to slam on his brakes. That causes congestion. Midas dissipates that effect. It tries to slow the whole motorway down a bit rather than having one area totally stopped.'

Tailgating. The root of all motorway evil. And it isn't very English, is it? We don't tailgate in a queue at the Post Office. We can get a bit pushy in the supermarket queue but that's only because we're under intense pressure to get all our stuff onto the conveyor belt before the till girl starts chucking it down the other conveyor belt. In all other walks of life, we are quite good at waiting our turn. We're not Italian.

'You're surrounded by a tin box,' he says. 'If you're in a queue for a cinema, you won't shove in because you're likely to get a thick ear. In a car, you are insulated. It stops the English being English.'

Rob's driving habits have changed since he started working at the control centre. 'My wife hated my driving. She wouldn't let me drive if she was in the car,' he says. 'She doesn't mind now so that's got to be a positive. Witnessing on a daily basis the effects of poor driving can be quite dramatic. I was shocked into driving bett—'

He was going to say '–er' but an important-looking phone in the middle of his flashy bronze-commander control panel starts ringing.

'Yup. Yup. Yup. Okay.' This is what he's trained for. It's a situation. Pinged up on the main video wall, we can see traffic is beginning to queue on the exit slip road at Junction 6. If the queue gets into lane one, everything will grind to a halt.

I look at the ceiling and scratch my ear while Rob gets on the phone to the road surface manager at Surrey Highways. Roadworks on the A22 are causing the tailback which is 'impacting our network'. The work was supposed to finish at four. It's now almost six. They've been top-dressing the dual carriageway and put a 20mph speed limit on both lanes.

'Can you pull rank?' I ask Rob as we watch the queue on the slip road worsen. He is bronze commander, after all.

'No.'

'But this is the M25. And it's about to grind to a halt because of a lazy man in a high-vis jacket with a bucket of tar. Can't you do some shouting?'

'I can stress the impact they're having. If this continues to cause congestion in the system, I will raise it to my boss [the silver commander who sits upstairs]. Then it will be discussed with the national liaison officer. Surrey Highways may fine the contractor for taking too long. Ultimately, they may consider not renewing their contracts.'

Hmm. But does that ever happen? Is there ever any impact?

'With the M25, yes. There's a huge amount of pressure for us to keep the M25 moving. The economic impact can be quite large.'

In the corner of the control room, the BBC traffic-bulletin woman is telling her listeners the bad news. 'Traffic is getting heavier at Junction 6 thanks to roadworks on the London Road.' Rob, a calm person even, according to his wife, when he's behind the wheel, admits that his blood pressure goes up a bit when he shuts a motorway. He tells me about the day he almost joined the queues up. 'There were a number of RTAs [road traffic accidents to those of you who haven't spent enough time watching *Traffic Cops*] and heavy congestions. Things quickly deteriorated and I had "Qs" around the whole screen.' Q means queue. Queue is bad.

'But it cleared up eventually. It always does. This will all be gone by half seven. All this will peter out.' We look at the slip road queue. We look at the hundreds of drivers slamming on their brakes because the bloke with the bucket of tar took a double lunch break. Midas is doing her best but humans have spoiled things today. Again.

'We're dealing with humans,' says Rob with a grin. 'No matter what system we have, we will always be relying on humans driving on roads and we don't do that properly. Until we do that properly we are always going to have collisions and traffic jams. Earlier today, we had a chicken house come off the roof of a car on the M3. We can't even tie things onto roofs properly.'

'We need driverless cars.'

'No, we just need to maintain a Zen-like patience when we're stuck in traffic. And that's easier said than done.'

On the way home, I'm sitting in the traffic jam Rob was trying to sort out (he was exaggerating, it hadn't all cleared by half seven). I try to be Zen. I say to myself, 'At least you're not in Sao Paulo. Sure the weather would be beautiful and the girls would be hot but you're married and it can take three hours to travel eight miles on the motorways around Brazil's largest city. One-hundred-mile mega jams are not unheard of and if you ask a Brazilian what they think about driving, they will moan even more than we do. And if I'd been travelling on the Beijing–Tibet expressway when they decided to do roadworks a couple of years ago, my two-hour commute would have taken nine days.

It doesn't help. The caveman instinct – fight or flight – is strong within me, master. I feel trapped. I feel gloomy.

This is England, congested, drizzly England. Nothing will change. We will always sit in traffic jams caused by selfishness, chicken hutches and lazy road workers. Motorways will never be fun. Motorway service stations are depressing. The end.

And then I hear an ethereal, magical voice. 'Go up north, Master Luke,' it says. 'High in the mountains, you will find the road clear and a service station you will want to write home about. May the force be with you.'

Driving way north on the M6, past the first bit of motorway at Preston, on and on for miles and miles, you eventually find yourself in Kendal Mint Cake country, the sort of landscape that gets geography teachers very, very excited. The Cumbrian fells are cold and windy and exposed and damp nine days out of ten but when the sun comes out you wonder why you would ever live anywhere urban. Or southern. Or busy. There is no traffic here. No tailgating Audis. No 'Congestion: please keep in lane.' Just the odd banger making a break for Gretna Green a few more miles ahead.

The Lune Gorge, just past Junction 38, bisects a fault line in the hills which join the Pennines and the Lake District fells. It is an ancient traveller's pass gone in a flash today. From there, the motorway curves and cuts north and, other than the fact that my Skoda is a little less likely to blow up at 65mph, this is as close to that original motorway driving experience as you can get today.

Between Junctions 38 and 39, Tebay services is 223 miles and light years from the motel on the M1 full of married people in PVC underwear spanking people who are not their husbands or wives. Instead of a Little Chef and a Travelodge, you get a farm shop, a café and a restaurant overlooking the Howgill fells. After a nice chat with an acne-free cashier, I order steak and ale pie, home-made using beef from the cows from that field yonder. It costs £8.50, not much more than a Whopper with Cheese Meal. The cashier doesn't ask me if I'd like to Go Large. Going large is not an option. The pie is served on an actual plate with an actual knife and an actual fork.

In the shopping area, there are no once-in-a-lifetime pic-nic chair/travel pillow/road atlas/windscreen-wiper fluid offers. There are no driving simulators in the games arcade so I can't pretend to do what I've just been doing for real for the last six hours. There is no games arcade at all. There is no mobile-phone-cable shop either and not one single person is trying to sell me a revolutionary new carpet-cleaning system.

There is a butcher busy dressing racks of lamb and slicing wild boar salami. There is a delicatessen so abundant that a group of Belgians are taking its photograph. There are organic cotton clothes and non-organic crampons. There are toys that are not made of plastic and do not beep in-discriminately. There is a whole section devoted to the professional pastry-making range of the Swiss company Kuhn Ricon and another section, of course, for Hunter wellies.

I buy some organic soap, an egg whisk, some wild boar salami and lashings of ginger beer. Then, with a last swig of strong coffee bought from an actual person, not a vending machine, I get back in the car and head to the beach.

10

THE BEACH

Though inland far we be,
Our souls have sight of that immortal sea
Which brought us hither.

WILLIAM WORDSWORTH, romantic

'NO, NO, NO. You've got it all wrong. You're just being a prejudiced southerner. Blackpool isn't anything like that. Well, okay, it is. But not the people. The people are great. Okay, not the people who go there. They are horrific, I'll give you that. Some of the things I've seen would make your eyes water. I'm talking about the people who live there. They are frontier people, pioneers, survivors, the best of the English. Go and see. I'll buy you a beer if I'm wrong.'

This from a friend called Steve who grew up just north of Blackpool and has long, curly Hucknall hair.* In retrospect, I should have discounted what he said from the off. But it was a romantic notion, the idea that Blackpool has been misjudged. And something about his little, pleading eyes poking out through his unkempt mop made it all sound entirely possible. Plus, this is the chapter in which we go on holiday. Bucket and spade. Sticks of rock. Can I have a flake in it, Dad, pllllease? Diving into the warm azure seas with the sun glistening on our muscly backs. No, not the last bit. But fish 'n' chips 'n' rock pools 'n' sandcastles 'n' futile wind-breaks 'n' futiler kites. The beach is close to our hearts. We are islanders after all. And if Steve was wrong, getting a beer off him would be worth the trip alone.

To the beach then, the place where we let it all hang out in its pale and fleshy glory. The English, stripped and at play, and all the class stereotypes come out. You've got the drug-addled offspring of the upper classes fornicating in posh bits of Cornwall, the middle classes snorting oysters in your Padstows, your Salcombes and your Whitstables and then you've got Blackpool which first started receiving holiday-makers in the 1720s, opened its first B&B in 1735 and was run-down and depressing by 1768.

* Slight exaggeration. It isn't ginger. On which note, did you see that news story about how a sperm bank is no longer stocking sperm from ginger people due to lack of demand. Mick Hucknall has a lot to answer for.

'The houses were few and scattered,' wrote Henry Banks sniffily in that year. 'From the hovel standing on the site of Bennet's Hotel to Fumbler's Hill, eight cottages might be numbered, all of them, with the exception of Forshaw's Hotel, merely huts: and at the lower end of Blackpool eighteen battered buildings, many of which are now washed down and the others dilapidated: these composed the village.'

We'll skip the intervening quarter of a millennium during which Blackpool became the north's foremost resort and even got its very own Eiffel Tower which, by the way, was very nearly called the Blackpool Eiffel Tower and is quite Eiffel-like. To prejudiced southerners, that was a mere blip. It has now reverted to type. It is as it was in 1768: battered buildings, washed down or dilapidated and most of the hotels are huts. That's the stereotype but what if my friend Steve Simply Not Red Hucknell was right?

He wasn't.

I arrived at lunchtime on a very out-of-season weekend in an attempt to give it a chance. If the people who come here are horrific but the people who live here aren't, then the off season, when no one was coming here and people were only living here, would be Blackpool at its best. Unfortunately, me and Blackpool got off to a bad start. Elsewhere in the country it was sunny and warm. The first daffodils were coming up, songbirds were rejoicing, bunny rabbits were playing leapfrog in the fields, and BBC weathermen were taking personal credit for the definite onset of spring.

In Blackpool, it was hailing. The only songbirds were drunk, hysterical and feather-free, their mottled blue flesh beginning to bleed heavily in the barrage of ice as they walked, arm in arm, along the promenade. There were eight of them in matching cowboy hats and they didn't seem to notice or mind the whelted skin, numbed as they were by the brutal temperatures and an afternoon's worth of booze. If I told you that their dulcet tones reminded me of *Le Chant des Oiseaux* by Clément Janequin, I'd be lying. One of the ladies had a boob hanging out. Another had a chip in her hair either by accident or for snacking on later.

But I wasn't going to jump to conclusions. That would be exactly the trap about which Steve had warned me. These were mere visitors, not locals – and they would be gone soon, dragged out into the Irish Sea by a freak wave or one of the ketchup-fed monster seagulls. What of the place itself? A beautiful Victorian seaside resort surely no more than a month or two off achieving World Heritage Status?

Still no.

I had booked a single room at a B&B ranked number three out of more than eighty on Tripadvisor's Blackpool hit parade so I was expecting something pretty damn special. Top 5 per cent and you're going to get a rainforest shower, a 26,000-spring mattress wrapped in 5,000-count Egyptian cotton sheets, and a breakfast the like of which can only be dreamt of somewhere less classy like Brighton.

I was disappointed.

The exterior of my number three B&B was reminiscent of a fallen-on-hard-times funeral parlour but inside it was distinctly less lively. My arrival went initially unnoticed so I wandered into the restaurant area beyond the lobby. It smelled strongly of formaldehyde, furniture polish and the grim futility of a thousand old-age pensioners. The owner, a no-nonsense woman in her early nineties, materialised and then dematerialised again without so much as a hello. For a moment, I thought she might have misunderstood my cheery hello for an attempted robbery and gone off to get her trusty meat cleaver. But I was wrong. Only a few hours later, she rematerialised with a room key and a seven-page registration form.

You remember *The Vanishing* – the original Dutch film, not the rubbish American remake – where the young Dutch cyclist gets abducted and her lover eventually tracks down the kidnapper? The kidnapper tells him the only way he can find out what happened to the girl is by drinking a cup of coffee laced with sedative. He does – and wakes up in a coffin six feet underground, and the movie ends. Shudder. That's exactly what my single room in Blackpool's third best B&B was like. The only real difference was that I had a window that looked out across an air-conditioning unit to a wall and a fire escape.

But it didn't matter. I was in Blackpool and Blackpool, according to Steve, was great. I went out and started walking north towards the Not Very Eiffel Tower, past the smartest mini golf course in Europe, a Sea Life Centre, a casino, a ghost train and a Travelodge which now seemed the height of luxury. Two hundred yards in, I realised I did not have the resilience of a northern hen party and I began to seek refuge. I could have had a meat salad at Tommy Duck's Pub but I decided instead to use my lunch money in the Lucky Star Arcade.

It took forty-eight minutes to lose £2.68 and gain £1.24 on the two-pence slots. If we were sitting a GCSE maths exam, I would now ask you to calculate the cost per minute of this classic English seaside entertainment. And you'd be tricked because the answer is 'Zero – because there is no entertainment. We're only here for the heating.'

Further along, the options for warmth become more drastic. There's Uncle Peter Webster's Pub ('Stag Parties welcome. Full English and a pint for £4.99' – breakfast of champions). There's a tattoo parlour ('We do not tattoo pregnant women'). There's the Original Gypsy Petulengro ('as seen in Spirit and Destiny'). And there's Sunseekers, offering tenner tans and fish pedicures, neither of which seemed appropriate. So I went all the way to the heart of Blackpool, into the Winter Gardens which are genuinely magnificent. There I settled in to watch the Invisible Middle Girl, Princes Arachnia, the Man Eating Fish, Miss Elasticina, the Headless Lady ('Alive and Human') but not the octogenarian ballroom dancers. You can have too much fun. Then I drank two pints, a large gin and another large gin and a pint to insulate against the cold and walked back to the B&B, past fifty other B&Bs, all of which looked worse than mine so maybe Tripadvisor was right after all. And at least it only smelled of formaldehyde.

'Few visitors remain a day or two in Blackpool without complaining of an offensive smell, especially perceptible to the inmates of the houses fronting the sea,' complained one writer during a visit in 1848. 'This proceeds from the effluvia of the house drains, which find vent both into the houses themselves and occasionally through outlets and openings near the cliff. It is, of course, a continual nuisance; but necessarily worst during the Blackpool season, from the heat of the weather, and the greater quantities of putrefying matter which find their ways into the drains.'

'Where's the best fish and chip shop?' I asked the no-nonsense nonagenarian, feeling newly grateful to be here in modern Blackpool with its modern facilities and modern hospitality.

'What?' She recoiled, as if I'd just asked if I could hold her close one last time.

'The best fish and chips? One where the locals go. Not tourists.'

'Down that way,' she creaked. 'On the bridge.'

For forty minutes, I walked around a bleak residential estate pockmarked with old people's homes wondering if the lady had heard me right. I smiled through a few windows, because I was still prepared to believe that Blackpudlians were wonderful, but no one smiled back. Several of those who blanked me were being force-fed their liquid dinner so you can't blame them. Everyone else? No excuse. You should always smile when a dark, gangly, half-cut man stares through your window on a stormy night as the wind rattles your PVC double-glazing. Always.

When I finally found the fish and chip shop, it was on a bypass, not a bridge and it was shut because it was 7.32 p.m. I went to the Co-op next door, bought an 'award-winning' sandwich, some wine and some crisps. And then I went back to the final scene of *The Vanishing* to fight my darkest fears.

By 8.30 p.m., I had warmed up enough to open the window. I could only budge it a few inches. By nine, I was too hot so I tried to budge it some more, failed and became even hotter as a result of my exertions. By half nine, I was feeling faint so I tried to turn off the radiator. Someone had removed the control valve, and, stupid me, I didn't have a spanner. By ten, I was a little panicky with the heat and the self-determinism of the radiator and the window so I downed the rest of the wine, had a cold shower, sorry, trickle (it's not like this in the rainforest), and went to bed.

By eleven, I was crying softly while trying to turn off the radiator using two pens and a pair of headphones. Soon after, I put a pillow on the windowsill and tried to fall asleep with my head squeezed through the gap. It was very uncomfortable so at midnight, I opened my emergency bottle of miniature whisky, stuck my legs out instead and finally, finally nodded off.

At one minute past midnight, I was awoken by the sound of a child telling another child to fuck off, and a man telling that fucking child to stop fucking shouting and the fucking child telling him to fuck off, and then all of them fucking laughing. The new guests were in the hall outside my coffin but my coffin was made of balsawood so the shouting was very, very close. And so was the party they then began to have.

At half past one, I opened the coffin and peered out, angrily because it was half past one and nervously because even after an hour and a half, it was hard to tell if the guests were fighting or enjoying themselves. I was confronted by a riot of viscose tracksuit, Tesco vodka, crew cuts, tattoos, gold chains and iPod speaker music.

'Would you mind keeping it down?' I asked menacingly.

They all laughed and, not for the first time, I cursed at my inability to be convincingly frightening.

'Yeah, sorry, mate,' said what I think was the mother but could have been the older sister or the grandmother.

'Thank you kindly,' I replied. Dammit. To make up for the politeness, I slammed the door except it was so thin it was like slamming a manila envelope.

'Thank you kindly,' mimicked the other guests. 'Haha-hahahahaha.'

The heating went off at 3 a.m. The party finished at 4 a.m. I fell asleep at 5 a.m. and woke with the next day's heating and the seagulls at half-six. I packed, I stormed downstairs, I told the nonagenarian that this was totally unacceptable and how on earth did she manage to make it into the top three of Blackpool B&Bs, and I left.

'Are you not having breakfast?' she said, with a genuinely concerned smile.

'No, thank you.'

I got five yards before noticing that my car was blocked in by a very large, very white, very black-windowed Range Rover with fluffy dice hanging from the rear-view mirror. It took half an hour to wake the relevant party animal and get him to move his pimped-up ride. I watched from a distance because it would be just my luck to get punched by someone I'd woken up early because I was trying to leave because that person had kept me awake all night. And then I was gone. I drove up through town, past the B&Bs boasting of 'lifts' and 'en suites' and 'central heating', past the tower, past Sunseekers with its fish condemned to a lifetime nibbling strangers' corns, and I would have kept going but Steve's annoying, little, nagging voice popped back into my sleep-deprived head.

'I'm talking about the place itself,' he said, all echoey and Lancastrian. 'The people who live there. Not the visitors.'

I would give it one last go.

I parked and stepped out onto the new sea defence, part of a £62-million regeneration project that has transformed the entire length of Blackpool's beach, only to make all the stuff behind it look even worse. It is beautiful, that great wave of stone holding back the ocean. Or trying to. In the early morning sunshine, grey seas battered the beach, cleaning away the footprints and buttockprints and cigarette butts of last night's endeavours. A plastic cowboy hat floated further out, all that remained of the cackling songbirds and really, in that moment, I had never felt more optimistic.

Our man from 1848 complained about 'the total absence of any regulations respecting bathing, and the consequent improprieties that are of a daily occurrence on the shore.' He doesn't want to describe these. 'It is sufficient to mention them; for they must be a matter of notoriety to everyone who has visited Blackpool.' He suggests an easy cure: 'Let separate bathing grounds be assigned to the two sexes, a quarter of a mile apart, clearly marked out by stakes or poles. It really is a disgrace to Blackpool that indiscriminate bathing should have so long existed there, when so simple a remedy would effectually put an end to it.'

Po-faced commentators have been missing the point of Blackpool for centuries. And I'm just the most recent. Last night, fun was had by all except me, and then it is morning and everything starts again. This is what makes the much derided old-school English seaside resort so special. It is, at least, optimistic, sometimes in spite of the odds.

I asked a woman walking her dog if there was anywhere good for breakfast and after she'd told me about a place way behind the seafront where only the locals go, she said, 'Do you like our Blackpool, then?'

No, obviously. But yes, now I'm not there any more.

PADSTOW, THOUGH. This has got to be more my cup of lapsang souchong. For a start, it never, ever rains in Cornwall. Second, you can spend a fortune on fish and chips that might not be as good as fish 'n' chips in a caff at the end of a pier but the fish is a posh kind and it's been pan-fried rather than dunked in hot, old grease. And us beach snobs love a gastronomic overspend almost as much as we hate getting sand in our loafers.

There is only one problem with Cornwall. It is a nineteen-day drive from anywhere else. In the era of the staging coach, it was a lot nearer but since the invention of the caravan, times have slacked off dramatically. You can get the train but that takes slightly longer and costs £3,792, not including the £48 boil-in-the-bag panini.

I flew. One hour. Only 1,000 fields. I counted. Roughly. England is small. You realise this when you fly over it. It just feels big down there because of all the traffic. Up here, I was almost relaxed, primarily because I had an allocated seat. In our pursuit of the perfect beach (and the most obscure city break), the English have embraced the pleasures of no-frills flying more than any other nation. We check ourselves in online, we queue for days and remove our belts and our shoes while sniggering security guards pick through our clear plastic bags of miniature pastes and potions.

'Is this your herpes simplex cream, madam?'

'Did you pack these nipple clamps yourself, sir?'

We have shared the 99p one-way-not-including-anything flights with stag parties and 6 a.m. pint-drinkers and we have seen the world, okay Europe, okay strange parts of Europe we didn't expect to see until we read the small print on our plane ticket. We have grown used to living out of one piece of hand luggage for a fortnight's holiday because it costs £400 to stick a bag in the hold. We have adapted. All is well.

Except when we haven't got an allocated seat.

To queue, as we have established earlier, is a great English skill. But where to queue? And when? On a no-frills trip, timing is everything and anxiety is hyperbolic. Queue too early and you're showing no decorum but queue too late and, well, that requires patience. So decorum is out and people, awful people, queue right from the off, before the off, sometimes before the gate has even been called. This is most upsetting for everyone else, except when it turns out the awful people have queued at the wrong bit. This can make a holiday.

Then you get on a bus and the whole structure and etiquette of the queue is thrown to the dogs. Which door to stand next to? Left or right? Back or front? Which stairs should we run up? Is it okay to climb over a fallen granny if she's clearly only a little bit bruised?

EasyJet, the second most soul-destroying of your no-frills options, has a system designed to play to our queue-based paranoia. Speedy-boarding: right up there with bear traps, reusable puppy drowners and the Fiat Multipla in my unofficial list of the world's vilest inventions.

When it started, you were effectively paying a premium to speedy-board the bus, after which it was back to a free-for-all for the plane. This caused riots, stand-offs and pink-faced men in linen blazers to shout, 'But I am a speedy-boarder,' so now the speedy-boarders speedy-board into a segregated speedy section of the bus like it's 1950s Alabama and they are better than us purely because of the colour of their money. Legitimising queue-jumping was a blow for Englishness. Even though easyJet has started dishing out set seats, we have them (and Chessington World of Adventures' fast track) to blame.

Flybe, on the other hand, had just given me my seat like it was no problem at all.

'Seat 10B. There you go, sir. Have a nice flight.'

I had my newspaper, detailing how two pilots from this very airline had been dismissed after squabbling all the way to Spain and not talking to each other on the way back. I had my inflight magazine with its thinkpiece on the prospects for Singapore as a place to build a business in the midterm as evaluated by the director of an international recruitment consultancy. (Prospects excellent, by the way. You should go right ahead.) And I had my Duty Free shopping brochure because I always like to impulse-purchase some perfume, aftershave, eyeliner, 'therapist's secret facial oil', a watch, a pair of sunglasses, a dual-sim mobile phone, a purse, a mouse shaped like a car, a plastic aeroplane and a life-balance wristband when I'm off to the beach.

Ah yes, the beach. I stepped out, with no life-balance wristband, into the wilds of Cornwall with its strange tropical vegetation, its clotted roads and its colonies of deadly false widow spiders, shipped over from the Canaries and now, by all (tabloid) accounts, prospering in the balmy conditions. It had been raining in London but here, it was socks and flip-flops weather, though of course still far too cold to swim. You can never swim anywhere outdoors in England, no matter how warm it is, what time of year it is or how many layers of wetsuit you are wearing, unless you are one of those eccentric septuagenarian grannies in black swimsuits and blue lips who insist it's good for the heart as they dive through the ice on New Year's Day. That is a fact.

Within the hour, I had reached the fabled port of Padstow, an enclave where middle-class herds roam free, taking Hipstamatic pictures of cutesy fishing boats, eating lobster, chugging Viognier (anything but Sauvignon Blanc, darling) and trying to explain the concept of tax avoidance to the Swedish au pair. I pushed through gaggles of open-necked, striped-shirted, pink-pullovered, green-loafered, be-chinoed, be-Botoxed long-weekenders to the nearest bakery for a snack. It was owned by Rick Stein of TV fame which was, as you can imagine, exciting but he wasn't there. He may not even have made the 100g of granola or the loaf of sourdough I purchased.

From Stein's bakery, I walked up the street, past Stein's Café, past Stein's Bed & Breakfast, past a notice telling me that Stein's Fisheries is located on the South Quay next to Stein's Fish & Chips, to a cutesy shop selling pointless clutter I could hand to my family by way of apology for not having taken them to the beach with me.

Stein's gift shop.

It sold Stein Wine, Stein Aprons, Stein Pestles, Stein Mortars and Chalky Dog Blankets. Chalky is a now deceased

Jack Russell who belonged to . . . Rick Stein. The only things it didn't sell were Stein stein glasses which seemed like a missed opportunity.

I bought a Stein tea towel, some Stein marmalade and a trinket that was either a boat fashioned from driftwood or driftwood fashioned from a boat. Or both. It was a rubbish souvenir but (a) it was one of the few things in Padstow that didn't have Rick Stein's signature on it and (b) who would ever want a good souvenir?

'I AM SICK TO DEATH OF PEOPLE ALLOWING THEIR DOGS TO "CRAP" ON THE PATH HERE,' says a sign outside a house just off the seafront. 'THE NEXT TIME THIS HAPPENS AND I CATCH YOU!, I WILL THROW A BUCKET OF DISINFECTANT OVER YOU!! AND I WILL!!'

This woman is on the edge. Look at all her exclamation marks. Note that final, mad, ranting 'and I will', the strained quotation marks around 'crap' – we are on the brink here. It's tempting to wait. It can't be long before one of the pink-shirted weekenders with his brogues and his schnauzer gets the disinfectant bucket. Imagine the YouTube hits.

The mad woman is not the only local to have reacted unhappily to the rise and rise of 'Padstein'. When residents protested at the disruption caused by building work on Stein's St Petroc's Hotel in 2007, Stein sent a tetchy letter to the protest leader. 'I have been very lucky to be able to promote my business and, of course, Padstow as well, through my books and television work,' wrote Stein. 'I would have been charmed if those other businesses that have benefited from the rosy glow of publicity, particularly those whose letting season has been considerably extended, could have shown some sort of recognition for the work done.'

He hasn't got everything. There is a shell shop that he doesn't own. But, as you would guess, it is a shop that focuses pretty much exclusively on the selling of shells and, as a sideline, things made out of shells. It is of absolutely no use if you are in the market for a vacuum-cleaner bag or a beach ball or an ice cream. Unless you want one made out of shells. Other than that? A lot of twee boutiques and an ice-cream van, not the middle-class dream but a middle-class theme park. It's laughing at us, not with us.

I escaped by passenger ferry to the other side of the Camel Estuary. It's not really an escape. It's out of the middle-class frying pan and into the upper-middle-class fire. Also known as Rock. Until 2008, this tiny resort was invaded each summer by partying toffs from Britain's poshest public schools. Every weekend, the calm sea air was spoiled by the braying, rutting, snorting cries of the progeny of the rich. Eventually, the local constabulary had had enough. It deployed the ultimate yoof-repellent, the Mosquito, a high-pitched alarm system that only young people can hear. I've tested a Mosquito in my local pub (for a story, not for kicks) and it is extremely effective. All the yoof had to leave after only a few minutes, unable to endure the irritating buzzing sound. The landlord was most displeased. And so it was in Rock.

Today, it was quiet, a blessed relief after Padstow. It still caters for the brat. There's a 'fabulously British' Jack Wills, a café doing jolly yum toasties, lots of rentable slate-and-velux beachfront properties. But the brat was not in evidence.

As I paused for a frappalatte, the peace was interrupted only by a minor argument between a convertible Merc and a very big Audi and another one between two Bugaboos. The pavements, as well as the roads, are not equipped for the London 4x4. Then I set off for what could easily be England's poshest fish and chips.

'Is this the right way to St Endoc Hotel?' I asked a passing Cornishman.

'You mean St Endonoc's,' he spat. Foreigners are not very popular on this side of the estuary either. 'There you are. Some free advice. Get that right and you're off to a great start.'

'Sorry, yes. Nathan Outlaw's place.'

'Place? Place? What do you mean place? It's a restaurant.'

He told me in the end, the miserable git. Nathan Outlaw's *place* is where people who used to go to Rick Stein's *place* go to escape all the Americans, according to a north Londoner called Chris who serves as chief adviser in all things beachy and pretentious. I could have had the tasting menu of roast brill followed by the crispy oyster followed by the salmon with sea lettuce followed by the monkfish and bacon with asparagus and pumpkin seed dressing followed by the Port Isaac crab with fennel and apple followed by the cod, the cheese and the burned rhubarb. And the chocolate meringue with peanut, yoghurt and orange. But it was lunch and I needed to be able to walk again later, so I went to the bistro for the lemon sole and chips.

There were no hen parties in. There were no partying gypsies. There was no Big Dipper or Little Dipper or donkey ride beyond the decking. There wasn't even any rock in Rock. Just me, some (very nicely cooked but otherwise uneventful) fish, some (very nicely stacked and you'd hope so for £3) chips and a room full of whispering couples. It all felt terribly genteel.

It wasn't. Not if you listened carefully.

'They're a shocking excuse for a family,' whispered the woman on the table behind me to the man who had a shocking excuse for a family. The man nodded non-committally which means he was a professional long-term relationship survivor. I didn't ask, it didn't seem the right time, but I'm guessing he's been doing this for at least twenty years.

'I like your mother but that thing with the flowers. I will never, ever be able to forgive them, Steve.'

Steve sipped his wine and made a sort of pigeon cooing sound. Total expert.

'I want you to confront them. I want you to shame them. I want them to know what they did.'

She really was sounding very *EastEnders*. I would have been panicking by now. Containment of the Whispered

Argument in the Posh Restaurant looked unlikely. The pigeon cooing could backfire and Steve could have a full-scale Scene in Posh Restaurant on his hands. Englishmen don't do Scenes, particularly in Posh Restaurants. But Steve was still in control. He ordered another bottle of wine.

'They're a shocking excuse for a family.'

She was on a loop. Shocking excuse. Flowers. Shame them. Excuse. Flowers. Shame. She never went into enough detail loudly enough to establish what the family had done with the flowers that required the shaming. Not sent them, presumably? Or sent them but to the other wife? Or dipped them in sheep blood, arranged them in the shape of a Harry Potter's scar and set fire to them outside a Busy Bees nursery? For a sense of completion, I should have asked but it didn't feel appropriate.

I left before them. For the next few days, I checked the nationals and the locals for Husband Stabbed with John Dory Bone in Two-Star Michelin Restaurant After Passive Mollifying Strategy Proves Ironically to Have Exacerbated the Situation. Nothing. Not even in the *Newquay Voice*. But I did have a conclusion, of sorts: people in Blackpool were having more fun than the people in Padstow were having more fun than poor old Steve in Rock.

ENGLAND HAS 1,150 miles of coastline and most of it is completely empty, but for the odd rambler. There are no purveyors of ice creams, no spiteful, privately contracted traffic wardens, no people beating each other with wind-breakers while their children throw stones at seagulls. It's strange that the English like to squeeze onto comparatively few bits of beach. With each other. I was always brought up to despise Other English People on Holiday. This is why we went to strange coastal places like North Wales or Thessalonica. The Rudds would seek out our bit of beach and then scowl at anyone who dared to intrude. Other English people manage to be more sociable. Not like the Italians, who are only happy when their towel is touching your towel, but still quite unEnglish. A strange sense of community infects people when they waddle out in their swimming trunks, enduring each icy wave with stoicism and yelping.

I would like to convince you of the virtues of the completely empty, completely pebbly,* completely rain-soaked beach. Somewhere out there is what makes living on this island special. But you either know or you don't know so we will move on to Whitby which is not empty at all but should

* Pebble or sand? It's as defining as bath or shower, dog or cat, sparkling or tap, ketchup or mustard, *X Factor* or *Strictly*, lager or bitter, toilet or loo, leg or breast, breast or bum. If you prefer the sandy beach, then I'm afraid you're in the shower/cat/breast/*X Factor* brigade. You are not a connoisseur. Most sandy beaches in England are brown and muddy, Heaney bogs, hard to lie on, unforgiving to kick a football around. The sand, when it does dry out, is there purely as an irritant, to spoil cucumber sandwiches, to go home with you in your socks. Pebble beaches, on the other hand, are much more interesting, providing you wear appropriate footwear and have a net for the rock pools and don't plan to go swimming or sunbathing or jogging.

be pretty moody. This is the place where Bram Stoker found inspiration for *Dracula*, where he imagined the Russian schooner *Demeter* washing into the storm-lashed harbour with no one on deck but a corpse of a girl. Well, *Dracula* might have been altogether chirpier if Bram had come here on a nice, sunny weekend in the summer. 'Despair has its own calms,' he wrote but so does a nice stroll under the cliffs to the fishermen's huts.

Whitby is half-Padstow, half-Blackpool with a North Yorkshire grin. You can pay £3 for a *Dracula* experience or £5 for ten Whitby scampi. Or £8 for both. You can see a fortune-teller or go on a mackerel fishing trip, drink micro-brewed beer in a Farrow and Balled gastropub or lose your candyfloss at Pleasureland. At Harry's Lounge Bar, you can eat lobster and chunky chips or moules frites. There are slow-moving grannies buying rock for their grandchildren while their children aren't looking. There are slow-moving dinkies buying fossil art in antique shops. The average level of fun is even higher than Blackpool. Steve from Rock would love it.

ON THE WALL of a greasy spoon in Croyde, north Devon, there is a handwritten note that reads: '*Live every day like your hair's on fire.*' Obviously it means this in the non-literal sense, not the grim, purgatorial sense. It's one of those schlock philosophies that works just as vomitously on a whiteboard in a management course as it does on the bumper of a forty-year-old campervan. Fortunately, the vast majority of us don't live every day like our hair is on fire. It would be exhausting, even in the non-literal sense. We live quite happily, quite uninflammably, on the sofa, on the train, on the motorway and on the swivel chair of our probably beige office. And that's more than enough to keep us going, thank you for asking.

I'm only ever in Croyde when I'm surfing and by 'surfing' I mean 'attempting to surf' and by 'attempting to surf' I mean 'trying not to drown under a large piece of fibre-glass with my feet tangled in the leash' and this happens about once every two or three or five years. In the normal grind of our unrelenting lives, my ageing surf buddies and I are not living every day like our hair is on fire. We have families and jobs and mortgages and logistical headaches and bureaucratic frustrations that prevent us having these magical hair bonfires.

When we arrive on the beach at Croyde with our little potbellies pipetted into our must-have-shrunk-in-the-wash wetsuits, we gaze out to the Irish Sea, the same sea that laps the swollen ankles of the women of Blackpool, and we take a deep, enthusiastic breath. We are English. We are at the beach. We are going to surf. We are totally living every day like our hair is on fire.

And then, six surfers in their teens, hair fully ablaze, run past us and steal the wave we weren't going to catch in the first place. And we give up and go to the pub.

THE BEDROOM

*When I came here, I couldn't speak a word of English,
but my sex life was perfect. Now my English is perfect
but my sex life is rubbish.*

JULIO IGLESIAS, sex bomb,
on moving from Madrid to Ramsgate

HERE WE ARE. We have arrived at the final stage of our journey. We have observed ourselves through the curtains at home, through the blinds at work and through beer goggles at the weekend. We're done. Almost. We just have to observe ourselves in bed. I'm sorry. We do. Stop looking at the ceiling. Stop fidgeting nervously. We must be brave and continental about this. No giggling. No swooning. We're all grown-ups and this needs tackling head-on. Hanky-panky. How's your father. Blanket hornpiping. Blowing the grounsils. Bonking. And so, of course, we must begin in Norfolk.

I meet Leo in the Sainsbury's car park on the outskirts of Thetford just before nine and we transfer into his clapped-out kidnapper's van. He is remarkably relaxed given the circumstances. I am quite nervous. I haven't done this before. He drives off up a country lane for a couple of miles and turns right down a dirt track. After about a mile picking the way through potholes and ditches, he kills the engine and we look around. Nothing. Nobody.

Back over the potholes in the failing light and onto the lane again, left, then right, then right again into a remote Forestry Commission car park. Thetford Forest, a patchwork of pines, heathland and broadleaves, provides the ideal setting for a day out, and a welcome refuge for a rich variety of animal and plant life, claims its website. But there's nothing happening here tonight either. Not even a pigeon.

We both pop a can of Red Bull and Leo swings the van back out of the car park, onto the lane, left, right, left, left, right. Another lay-by. Another car park. Another unmarked clearing in the woods. Nothing. He's getting frustrated. Forty minutes have passed and darkness is almost upon us. Where is everybody? But this is what I expected.

Dogging, the rural act of having sex in the back of Volvos while other people watch, is an urban myth, a tabloid fantasy, a big, throbbing exaggeration. It just doesn't tally with the English reputation for reserve, especially when it comes to sex.

'It's a bit early,' says Leo. 'And I haven't been up here for a few months. Maybe they've moved.'

'Or maybe it doesn't happen? Just like I said.'

This spurs him on. Left, right, right, left, left. Another car park. It's 9.45 p.m. now, pretty much dark. Not the time you would expect to see a lot of people out and about. But the car park is busy, suspiciously busy.

'Bingo!' says Leo.*

There are three cars in one corner, four cars in another and six in a circle by a bench. People, mostly men, are standing around in wax jackets chatting. Some are just walking around on their own. Doggers, perhaps. Or just dog walkers.

'No, they're doggers.'

'But they're not doing anything. They're just milling about.'

'That's what happens. They all chat for hours. Then, at some point, something just happens and they all start doing it.'

'I don't believe you.'

Slap, tickle, bang in the middle of the car park is a vintage Mercedes Benz motorhome beside which two septuagenarian couples, all blue rinse and *Reader's Digest* subscription, are having an elaborate picnic supper. There are high-back picnic chairs, a large table, a murder of Tupperware, the general paraphernalia of elderly campers.

'If you're right, these poor old tourists are going to be in for the shock of their lives.'

---

* Leo is not a dogger. He is supposed to be making a programme about doggers. This is difficult if doggers are a figment of tabloid imagination.

'Maybe they're here for the dogging too?'

'Don't be disgusting.' (Leo is frequently disgusting.) 'They're in their seventies. That one has a limp.'

'Well, why else would they be having a picnic in a car park in the middle of Norfolk at ten at night?'

There are so many reasons I can think of before I reach 'because they're doggers'. They could be celebrating an eightieth birthday or a golden wedding anniversary. Or readying themselves for a night of astronomy or owl spotting or badger baiting or bridge. They could be having an overnight stop on their way from Suffolk to Derbyshire or Northumberland to the Dignitas Clinic. The one in the plaid shirt with the varicose veins looks a bit peaky. Before I have a chance to list all the things four old people can do in Norfolk before having a public gangbang, Leo has got out of the kidnapper's van and is now chatting to one of the roaming men.

'All right.'

'All right.'

'Nice evening.'

'Nice evening.'

If this is dogging, and I still can't believe it is, this is how it begins. Chatting about the weather. Their voices carry away in the night air, lost among the trees and other murmured conversation, and I am alone in the van with my thoughts. Nothing is confirmed. The evidence is a long schlong short of incontrovertible. Another man – mid-fifties, red-wine complexion, ferrety eyes, possibly holding his penis in his hand – leans in from the darkness through the passenger window and I look back threateningly. Nothing to see here, mate.

'All right,' he grunts.

'All right,' I reply.

'Nice evening.'

'Yup.'

He grunts again and wanders off. Probably just a twitcher looking for his friend, another twitcher, who was probably just waiting in exactly the same sort of van as I happened to be in. These things happen.

A plump-lipped girl in the passenger seat of a Citroën is laughing hysterically at something a man standing at her door has just said. Two other men are standing a few feet behind him, looking alert. Probably just the daughter of a Russian oligarch chatting to a fellow Ipswich University geography student about the field trip they've been on today while her security detail stand guard. The security detail don't have earpieces though and they aren't wearing dark suits either which is odd.

All the time, cars come in and out of the car park, circling round like sex-pest sharks. They're looking for action, Leo would say. Or just a nice quiet place to take a break, I would reply. But Leo isn't here. Where is Leo? Leo? LEEEOOO?

A Passat, not a Volvo, parks up about twenty yards from our van. A suspiciously blonde, suspiciously big-breasted woman in her late twenties steps out in an eye-wateringly short skirt. Her husband/partner/business colleague, early forties, gets out as well. He's all dolled up like he's about to go on a night out in Norwich with the lads. Jeans, white shirt, hair gel. They start talking to each other by the driver's door. Three men from different corners of the car park swoop in and join them.

'All right.'

'All right.'

'All right.'

People in Norfolk are probably just friendly. The grannies and granddads are tucking into a perfectly constructed raspberry pavlova which, at the very least, says something about the quality of their campervan's suspension (of which, horrifically, more later).

After a few more minutes, the blonde climbs back into her Passat and re-emerges a few minutes later in thigh-high boots and a coat. That's it. Underneath, there is just the flash of flesh. Still no full-on confirmation but, well, it's looking quite good. Or bad. Depending on the newspaper you read. And meanwhile, blissfully unaware, the elderly tourists are packing away their picnic and getting ready for an early night and at long last, Leo is back with a big grin and bigger news.

'They are doggers,' he says, pointing at the campervan as one of the grandpas, the one with the limp, pulls the curtains closed.

'Shut up.'

'They've been coming up here for years. Old-school. Used to be up here all the time. Now, only rarely. And these days, they do their stuff in private.'

For a while, everything stands still. The world is paused in this horrific and yet strangely enlightening moment. Horrific because it's a granny orgy. Strangely enlightening because, well, good on them. If I'm having a raspberry pavlova followed by group sex when I'm seventy-five, I'll be amazed. Then, the campervan starts to creak a bit. The lights are out inside but there is giggling. And then, no . . . I can't write it down. The therapist says I must put it behind me. I need to move on.

Elsewhere in the car park, the mood swings from anticipation to boredom to anticipation to boredom. There are about thirty people here, still in different factions, milling about, pretending milling about is perfectly normal. They can't all be here because 'it's a nice night for a bit of fresh air'. Having arrived sceptical, I'm now impatient. If you're here to dog, what's with all the chatting? Get on with it. But no, the blonde is chatting. The oligarch's daughter is chatting. A whole group, five mid-fifties blokes, three mid-forties women, in the far corner is chatting. Men keep looking through the windows at me and Leo, before walking away, disappointed. I would be too. Here I am in a kidnapper's van in a dogging spot in deepest, darkest Norfolk and all that's going on is chatting.

And then, some time near midnight, whole hours after everyone arrived, something changes. The mood swings. The Russian oligarch's daughter who I'm now pretty certain isn't a Russian oligarch's daughter begins to fellate the chap with whom she was chatting through the passenger window.

The security detail do absolutely nothing but watch. Then one of them takes his turn. Others gather to watch.

Three cars along, the blonde is flashing at the other men and playing with her suspiciously large boobs while her husband looks on, totally unbothered. Right in the middle, the campervan has stopped creaking and the lights are back on. One of the filthy grandpas is making a brew while the filthy grandmas put their teeth back in.

Next, the blonde gets into a different car with a man who is not her husband. Three men get into the Passat with her husband. Another car fills up behind them and they all head off in convoy.

'They're going somewhere more private,' says Leo. 'We could follow but it might be a bit . . . weird. What do you think?'

'No,' I reply.

'Okay,' says Leo.

'No,' I repeat, because the fine balance between curiosity and a deep sense of toe-curling embarrassment has now tipped heavily towards the latter. And also, there is powerful etiquette to dogging. We're not in the gang. Following them would cross a line. 'Let's go back to Sainsbury's.'

Dogging actually happens. But it doesn't happen the way you'd think it would happen if you ever thought about it, which of course you don't. It isn't a wham-bam-thank-you-mam fumble in the jungle. Well, it is but only after a whole social thing. Take these people out of the woods and put them at the end of a train platform and you've got train spotters. Put them in a church hall, and you've got a flower-arranging society. Same desire for friendship, tribalism, commonality and sense of belonging. Same conversations even.

How's the weather?

How's work?

Is this your first time here?

I like the way you've trimmed your bush.

If dogging happens in Italy or France, or more imaginably, Finland, I'm sure it wouldn't be quite so . . . nerdy. Anoraky. Reserved. Like someone's about to fire up a spreadsheet or record something in a logbook or call a point of order at any moment.

THE MOST EXCITING THING that has happened in our bedroom in the last few years took place on a Monday last November. We upgraded our duvet. It might not sound exciting but it was more exciting than sitting in Leo's van waiting for Norfolk people to have stranger-sex, I can tell you. This was the final upgrade of the Englishman's three-stage Duvet Transition Model (DTM). It is an important stage of life, full of deeper meanings and contentment but, at the same time, melancholy.

DTM Stage One happens when you first leave home and you are in John Lewis with your mum and she buys you a duvet because you've spent all your money on cider and a room in a shared flat which has damp and thin walls and probably cockroaches. The duvet will be strictly utilitarian. Priorities are ease of maintenance (for example, how soon will the duvet begin to smell if you're always putting still-damp covers on them?) and price, but not necessarily in that order. No geese will have contributed to its making. It's duck if your mum is posh, synthetic if she isn't, and away with you to your bachelor twenties.

But then you meet the person with whom you intend to spend the rest of your life. She is the one, probably because you're both at that age and the roulette wheel just happened to stop but also, hopefully, because she is the girl of your dreams. But. Duvet One. Its days are numbered. Like an unappreciated yet fiercely loyal Labrador in a house recently taken over by a dog-hating, controlling, evil step-mother, it must go. It has seen too much. It has wagged its tail at other women. DTM Stage Two. You go to John Lewis with your control freak, not your mum, and buy marriage bedding. Now we're talking duck down. Or, at a stretch, goose feather or, if everything has gone well in your world, goose down. Mould-resistance is less of an issue. Longevity is. We went for goose feather. Our marriage got off to a wonderful start.

Stage Three is infinitely more complicated and expensive. Until this winter, I didn't even know it existed. But it does. It is the stage where you realise that the most important thing going on in the bedroom and possibly life is a good night's sleep. You have already got the right number of pocket-sprung springs in your mattress. You have thousands of Egyptians counting in your sheets. Now it all comes down to the type of goose.

'Is it that important?' I ask Julie from John Lewis, who has been to the factory where they make the duvets and she can personally vouch for the quality.

'It does make a difference and they really are fantastic quality,' says Julie.

'I'm sure that's the case, Julie. But what I'm worried about is the goose. What is the difference between the winter snow goose, the Siberian snow goose and the Hungarian non-snow goose?'

'The winter snow geese are harder to find,' she says. This is interesting but not that helpful. I don't want to be paying an arm and a leg for a duvet because it was harder to get the geese into it, although I do appreciate the effort. The winter snow goose lives in the remote Altai Mountains, an inhospitably glacial environment on the borders of Russia, China, Mongolia and Kazakhstan. Imagine the goose's surprise when a man from John Lewis turns up with a big net and a pair of eyebrow-pluckers.

'Right. But in terms of user experience?'

'It's the loft.'

'The loft?'

'Yes, the loft.'

Right. The loft. Fill power. Fluffiness, basically. Fill a duvet with duck down and it'll be heavy and warm or thin and not so warm. Fill it with the innermost coat of an Altai Mountain snow goose and it will be warm and thin.

Wife and I discussed this intoxicating prospect for maybe a month: the pros ('but it will be so light and yet warm, darling'), the cons ('how will it make the Hungarian geese feel?'/'it's only a bloody duvet'). And then we bought it anyway. And it is very light and very, very warm. Far too warm for anything that (a) isn't a goose and (b) doesn't live in the Altai Mountains. But still, the whole experience was very, very exciting.

BETWEEN THE RELATIVE EXTREMES of dogging and duvet-buying, what really goes on in the English bedroom? It is, after all, the most important room in the house, the place where we sleep and do things other people do in Forestry Commission car parks. The trouble is, we have this rather persistent reputation for prudery. Anywhere else on the Continent, it's sex first, then a cigarette, then more sex, then maybe a little ride around town on a moped without crash helmets, then sex again. Here, received opinion is that we'd rather not talk about it, let alone do it, thank you very much. On average, the French have sex 120 times a year. The English can't even muster 100.* The French are Pepe le Pew. The English are Winnie-the-Pooh. Not tonight, Eeyore. I'm having a nice cup of tea with Christopher Robin.

In a global sex survey, conducted by onepoll.com, Englishmen are accused of being the second worst lovers

* It's ninety-two but I'm rounding up.

on the entire planet. Laziness or 'letting the women do all the work' was the principal criticism among the 15,000 women who took part in the survey. The only men worse than the English were the Germans who were considered 'too smelly' which seems very harsh. Spanish men came on top, so to speak, closely followed by Brazilians and Italians.

Now, I don't know where they found 15,000 women with not just the experience to judge multinational sexual prowess but also the willingness to talk about it. It isn't important. Polls come, so to speak, and polls go. What these women need to realise is that Englishmen are working against centuries and centuries of repression. It's a wonder we manage to have sex at all.

Until the eighteenth century, marriage was usually based not on important things like cup-size or personality but on the number of fields or pigs bundled into the bargain. Not sexy. Then came the Era of Politeness which was a step forward, but only a little step, not a giant leap. In a society attempting to become more socially and culturally aware, men were encouraged to understand women's feelings. They did this in a typically un-understanding way – by fawning over them, opening carriage doors and throwing coats in muddy puddles. In return, the women were merely expected to be perfect, passive porcelain dolls. And not in any way give the suggestion that they liked sex. Sex was for having babies, not fun.

'Marriage is the highest state of friendship,' declared Samuel Richardson in *Clarissa*, a very long novel about a young woman's quest for virtue.

'Boring,' shouted the odd libertine. 'Show us your knickers.' But those rare, naughty voices were drowned by a tide of early modern Mary Whitehouses.

One of the biggest publishers at the time was the thoroughly joyless Society for the Promotion of Christian Knowledge,* established in 1698 in association with the equally loveless Societies for the Reformation of Manners and, by the early 1700s, it was knocking out alarming tomes on why masturbation, mutual masturbation, female orgasm and other sexual exploits were dangerous, evil or just plain rude. In the bestselling page-turner *Onania* or *The Heinous Sin of Self Pollution, and All its Frightful Consequences in Both Sexes*, male readers were informed that touching themselves would cause gonorrhoea, stranguries and priapisms as well as the distinct possibility of fainting fits. Women would risk hysteria, barrenness and imbecility. Hundreds of readers wrote in thanking the society for saving them from these horrors.

Even King George III got in on the tut-tuttery, publishing a proclamation 'For the encouragement of Piety and Virtue, and for the Preventing and Punishing of Vice, Profaneness and Immorality'. The short version? If you could all

---

* Still going today, though the 'Propagation' has been changed to 'Promotion' and they're less freaked out by masturbation.

refrain from having fun, we'd be most awfully grateful, what what.

Then came the Victorian era, which was hardly any less prudish. In church every Sunday, and Wednesdays too, congregations were warned of the dire consequences of giving in to the temptations of the flesh. While men worked off their sexual frustration by building bridges and railways and the empire, women, even aristocratic ones, didn't. 'Once married, the perfect lady did not work; she had servants,' writes the historian Martha Vicinius. 'She was mother only at set times of the day . . . her status was totally dependent upon the economic position of her father and then her husband. In her most perfect form, the lady combined total sexual innocence, conspicuous consumption and the worship of the family hearth.' No wonder so many of the great nineteenth-century novels were so tense.

Frolick forward another 100 years and you have the Pill, the Rolling Stones and, gag, people my parents' age all having sex with each other and doing the twist and driving around in Minis wearing minis. But the Really Swinging Sixties wasn't enough to shake England's prudish reputation. For the last forty years, shorthand for us in bed has not been sex, drugs and rock 'n' roll. It's been *No Sex Please, We're British*, a film that came out in 1973. A film starring Ronnie Corbett playing an assistant bank manager. A film that comprises a lot of people getting in a complete state because some pornographic photographs get delivered to the wrong address.

I had never seen this film before, only read headline variations on its title on a daily basis, and used it myself once for a column about sock drawers. I ordered it. It arrived in a manila envelope, much like, hilariously, Ronnie's porn. By hilariously, I mean not hilariously. *No Sex Please, We're British* is not funny. I doubt it was funny in 1973 but was it representative? Were the English quite so shockable then? Surely an assistant bank manager, even a Barclays one, would just chuck the porn in the bin or give it to his single mates?

As for the actual history of sex, you could take an entirely different walk through the centuries if you wanted. During the 'polite' eighteenth century, there were plenty of impolite people listening to erotic manuals being read out loud in alehouses. You don't even get that in Wakefield these days. Homosexuality was all the rage in the Molly Houses of London, as was contraception in the ever-so-off-putting form of sheep bladders sold on street corners around Covent Garden. George III's proclamation for the encouragement of piety could be seen as a reaction to all the lack of piety. Please, loyal subjects, if I may be so bold, can you all stop looking at pornography and do some work, what what what?

In the Victorian era, the temptation that was supposed to be resisted at all costs just wasn't. An extraordinary survey of forty-five randomly selected mostly middle-class Victorian women conducted by Dr Clelia Duel Mosher, the most mind-bogglingly named feminist ever, reveals that sex wasn't quite as functional a chore between man and wife as the various societies for the upholding of boringness would have liked. Three-quarters of the women surveyed actually desired sex, more than half felt that pleasure for both sexes was a reason for intercourse and three-quarters did it at least once a week.

'It is a very beautiful thing, and I am glad nature gave it to us,' said one of the respondents. Not exactly Woodstock (other respondents said they had taught themselves about sex from 'watching farm animals') but this is fifty years before Alfred Kinsey began asking everyone in Indiana about sex. And more than eighty before Ronnie Corbett got his knickers in a twist in a film by which we are totally, probably unfairly, defined.

WHERE ARE WE TODAY on the togging-to-dogging scale? Are we like the naughty Victorians or the nice ones? Are those 15,000 jet-setting harlots wrong or are Englishmen really the second-worst lovers in the ENTIRE WORLD, including Moldova, Vanuatu and the Vatican?

In order to find out, I went all Dr Clelia Duel Mosher myself. I conducted my own survey in which I asked Englishmen and women not to compare Russians with Swedes with the French with bloody Brazilians. Instead, I asked them to talk frankly about their own English bedroom, and what goes on in it. Warts and all. Hopefully not actual warts but no holes barred. Figuratively speaking. In return for their unflinching honesty, I promised anonymity.

The survey was posted online and widely circulated. Viral, you might say. Within one week, almost 400 English people had spilled the beans. Of those who met the criteria of Englishness, some had been quite brief and prudish about it – which is not only to be expected but also to be applauded. Without a bit of reticence, you're only a fake tan and a vacuous outlook on life short of *The Only Way is Essex*. Others were less demure. Others still wrote whole essays on the most intimate aspects of their sex lives, using the survey as a confessional box or a therapist's chair. And now, exclusively, we are going to share the intimacy with you lot, complete and utter strangers. We will find out if we're closer to the dogging extreme than the duvet-discussing one.

Of the 376 people who responded, 30.9 per cent have sex less than once a month; 13.4 per cent do it 'about once a fortnight'; 17.2 per cent manage about once a week; 26.6 per cent are at it twice a week; and a hardcore 8.4 per cent ticked the 'daily' box. They aren't even the most rampant. An entirely outrageous minority of 3.4 per cent of actual English people living in England sleeping with other English people in English bedrooms ticked, 'Sometimes more than daily – we're at it like rabbits.' Well done them.

Unfortunately, this means that the largest group, at just under a third, is the 'less than once a monthers' – very much in line with our Ronnie Corbett reputation. Very unBrazilian. Very *je ne sais rien*. But. Do not be disheartened. For starters, 28.1 per cent of respondents are 'between relationships'. Some of them will, of course, be dating. Some of these daters might even be, how you say, tarty. They might have all the *Sex and the City* box sets. They might even think Samantha was a bit of a prude. But most of those 'between relationships' are managing to spend their time not between the sheets either. Of those in relationships, more than 96 per cent are at it at least fortnightly. Well done, all of you.

Let's drill down a little further, so to speak. Three-quarters of respondents have sex more or less exclusively in the bedroom, although 19.1 per cent of them used to be more geographically adventurous. The remaining quarter claim to know no such confines, doing it in the bedroom 'but quite often in other parts of the house' as well. Wild. Two of the 376 respondents have sex in their sex dungeon. Either that or two people filling in this survey were pulling our . . . leg.

We can be happy with this. It is not disastrous. Beds are comfortable. Kitchen worktops are not. That's just a fact. But what effect does familiarity have on our love lives? Does longevity breed early nights and boredom? Let us compare those fortunate enough to be in new relationships with those . . . fortunate . . . enough* to be in very old relationships. It isn't great news. Almost half of those respondents enjoying the first six months of new love claim to be having sex on a daily basis. Some of them for most of the day.

'We have both recently just come out so we're experimenting with everything we've read about lesbian sex,'

---

* She might be listening. Read between the lies, sorry lines.

writes one happy customer. 'It's fantastic and lasts for hours, and it's the most satisfied I've been for years.' It isn't just the lucky lesbians. All the newbies, regardless of age, sexual persuasion or even bedroom wall colour (an admittedly less exciting part of the survey) are at it at least once a week.

'Satisfying.'

'Very satisfying.'

'Incredibly satisfying.'

'God, it's so satisfying.'

'It still feels so new . . . he's been away for a bit so we have discovered that Skype can help keep everything simmering.'

'We spend most of the time wanting to rip off each other's clothes.'

'My partner loves nice lingerie* so Agent Provocateur is a must,' explains one. 'I also invested in hand ties, a whip and a tickling feather. He makes me feel confident so I'm happy to give new things a try.' Next stop, Thetford.

For those in longer-term relationships, this could all be seen as quite grating. Do these people have no regard for the heinous sin of self-pollution, and all its frightful consequences in both sexes? But it suggests that English people, at least in the first flush of love, can experience passion, excitement, liberation and an almost continental *joie de vivre*.

'Mind-blowing. Our connection is incredible . . . we also have that intimacy with each other and love cuddles.'

---

* Must be a Brummie if that naughty shopping centre is anything to go by.

Enough already. What about grumbles? Well, I've scoured the questionnaires with a fine toothpick and they are, to say the least, minor. One respondent complained of initial mechanical issues (swiftly overcome). Another pleaded for all twenty-something men to be re-educated that not all women are as bald as Barbie. Generation Y is also Generation Internet Pornography. And that was about it.

In the six-month-to-two-year relationship window, the honeymoon is far from over but the rabbits do calm down a little. Half of men claim to have maintained their daily sex workout but women, perhaps more truthfully, report a slackening of the pace. About 73 per cent make love at least twice a week, 15.4 per cent have dropped to once a week and a statistically significant though psychologically gratifying number have slipped to 'fortnightly' or 'less than monthly'. The complaints, on the other hand, were creeping in. 'We've gone from sex daily and in unpredictable places (kitchen, parents' living room, etc.) to once a week and in bed,' writes one. 'Sex is good but mostly predictable, spiced up on special occasions.'

'As I've got older (thirty now; death imminent), I've found that it's the men who are responsible for our reputation,' suggests another, very sweepingly. 'The older they get, the less imaginative and more uptight they become. I think a woman will do whatever her man wants her to do (I draw the line at roaring – yes, that actually happened) but men have become a caricature of the stiff-upper-lipped Brit.'

'I am hornier than he is but he likes more acrobatic stuff than I do.' Okay.

'I'm simply his fling on the side, a fling that's been going on for two and a half years now.' Umm.

'It's changed but passion is still there when we're not pooped from the working week.'

Overall, the moaning-moaning is still outweighed by the other sort of moaning. It is outnumbered by pages and pages of really quite impressive sexual experimentation. There are tickling feathers, blindfolds, dominance, submission, sex toys, more sex toys, fantasy role-play. I'm censoring for the benefit of those who prefer to remain floating in the serene, undisturbed calm of their Victorian prudery but I'm beginning to doubt there are many of you still out there. It's official. The English, at least in the first two years of a relationship, are at least 84 per cent filthy. There have even been accidents, some of them quite extensive.

'We've just moved in together,' explains a not-sheepish-enough respondent. 'Had my boyfriend not sustained a relatively serious injury to the penile area some months ago on an over-enthusiastic weekend, we would be at it like bunnies. I do rather hope he recovers sooner rather than later.'

The poor guy. Lying there with his broken penis, splinted and plastered, his terrifying dominatrix of a girl-friend standing over him, tapping her watch with her leather-gloved hand. Is this what England is really like? Is it just me with the duvets?

No. It may well be different in your Spains, your Moldovas and your Papua New Guineas but in England, and you might want to hold the front page for this, people who are lucky enough* to be in a relationship for more than ten years have less sex than people who have not reached the two-year mark. I know.

Most of the respondents in the ten-year-plus bracket are in their thirties or forties. Almost 90 per cent of them are married. These are the middle-agers, the middle-of-the-roaders, the silent majority, the parents, the exhausted, huddled masses for whom the impulsive, carefree excitement of youth has been replaced by the careful certainty of decline. Only 2.1 per cent of them are still at it on a daily or more-than-daily basis;** 45 per cent are managing the once- or twice-a-week bracket; 21 per cent are down to every other Saturday; and 31.5 per cent have sexy time less than once a month. This is getting into birthdays-and-anniversaries territory.

'We know what works and we stick to it,' writes one woman.

'Boring. Lost its spark and at fifty I can't believe I might not experience serious lust again,' writes another.

---

* She still might be listening.

** If you need help with sex addiction, contact Dr Thaddeus Birchard, snigger, at the Marylebone, snigger, Centre. His programme has 'helped treat people with compulsive patterns of sexual behaviour for over ten years'.

'Quite satisfying.'

'Not very satisfying.'

'I adore sex, the dirtier the better,' writes another still, raising hopes. 'But we've been together for fifteen years now. Work kills us, we're both a bit tubby these days and too knackered most of the time. We generally only have sex when we're blind drunk and assured of a lie-in the next day. It's a very sad state of affairs.' Hopes dashed.

'It has become infrequent, but when we do have sex, we seem to follow a set pattern, and I am very disappointed that oral sex is off the menu since marriage.' That was a bloke, of course.

'We used to be tri-weekly,' writes another, plagiarising the Big Book of Hilarious Anniversary Speeches.* 'Now it's more try-weekly. One day, we will transgress to the third stage: try weakly.'

There are solutions, though not necessarily the ones you might get from a marriage counsellor.

Solution one: 'I love my husband and still find him very attractive but I will confess that I have become sexually re-vitalised since becoming a Rafael Nadal fan five years ago. In my head I picture a hard, naked Rafa making love to me and I'm good to go. That's not something I feel the need

---

* Which is not yet in existence although a man called Michael Davenport has written a book called the *Instant Anniversary Speech* which is available for just £1.99 on the Kindle and promises to help you create a speech so brilliant it will be remembered for years.

to share with my husband. I would hate to upset him and I'm pretty sure knowing I'm fantasising about Rafa wouldn't make him happy.'

Solution two: 'In 2006, I started a four-year affair with a man twenty years younger than me which really invigorated my interest in sex. Fortunately my husband fought for me and now we have made a conscious effort to restore our sex life and although "not better than ever" it is certainly very good again.'

Solution two again: 'I married a long time ago to my first boyfriend. I recently took a lover who enlarged my sexual knowledge considerably. What fun that was. Now I would consider myself to be well-versed in sexual shenanigans but unfortunately my husband is not. We still manage to have fun.'

And solution two yet again, this time quite shoutily: 'You seem to assume that I and other respondents only have one sexual relationship on the go. As it happens, I have had a lover for the past four years (as well as a husband I love too). Should I do this survey twice? It's great with both but not a lot can beat the thrill of sliding out for a day-room tryst at an airport hotel with the lover.'

'That's my one,' says Wife, straight-faced.

'Haha,' I reply.

'No, seriously,' still straight-faced. 'I do love you but I'm off to Gatwick.'

'Hahahahahaha.'

And then there is no solution at all: 'When your husband tells you after nineteen years of marriage that he is transgendered and has never fancied women, it not only explains a lot of things that you believed were your fault but also virtually eliminates any chance of getting what you need elsewhere. At sixty-two, all one is left in my case with is do-it-yourself; in his he goes to clubs and has a more exciting social life. (We don't want to divorce.)'

None of this paints a particularly rosy picture of marriage. But overall, it's not that bleak. Only just ever so slightly more than half of the relationships can be categorised somewhere between irredeemably bad ('terrible', 'wish it were more adventurous', 'more meat and two veg than spicy takeaway') to something not that bad at all. The upper end of this group, this long-term relationship middle ground, is the area we might define as stereotypically English, summed up by a phrase repeated no fewer than six times in the survey: 'We have a routine.' I am proud to say that everyone else, nearly half of the ten-year-plus brigade, report positively. There are lingering signs of passion, satisfaction, adventure and even mild bondage. They've still got it. Hurrah!

And you can worry too much about sexy sex. What about something a bit more meaningful? I bet Winnie-the-Pooh went on to have better long-term relationships than Pepe le Pew. Piglet and he will be lifelong friends. Christopher Robin? Maybe more. You can't say that about Monsieur Le Pew and Penelope Pussycat. We have grounding, commitment, mutual respect as well as mutual sarcasm. In the decade-long relationships, there are affairs, abstinence and the decline of physical affection but also, overwhelmingly, there is love.

'Less sex as we get older but we talk more.'

'Very loving, sexy and satisfying.'

'Probably not as wild and frequent as it was in the early years (you can blame the kids for that) but loving, committed, happy, and still surprising from time to time.'

And my favourite: 'I feel like I'm a lucky man. My wife is beautiful and I'm less intimidated by her looks as time goes by (she's still a fox).'

'I wrote that one,' I tell Wife.

'No, you didn't,' she would have said if she hadn't been at Gatwick.

And what about all the other things that happen in the English bedroom besides canoodling, not canoodling and sleeping? Such as television-watching? On this, the nation is divided evenly between those who will absolutely never have a television in the bedroom so help them God (because it really is the end of any chance of ever having any sex life again if you can just flick a switch and find a smirking Jeremy Paxman in the room with you) and those who do.

We are less divided on bedroom wall colours. The choice of shades ranges from the predominant magnolia right across to calico, a light buttery colour which is slightly darker than magnolia. Our sheets are cotton, not silk, but sometimes Egyptian. I didn't ask about duvets. Two fifty-somethings have ceiling mirrors. One of them admits the time might have come to get rid of it, which couldn't sum up England any better if it tried.

'That's late for the phone to ring.'

'Just leave it.'

'What if it's important?'

'It won't be. Come on, let's go to bed. It's Tuesday and everything.'

'There it goes again. I'm going to answer it.'

'Oh for goodness—'

'It was my sister.'

'Has someone died?'

'It's only nine. Are the kids asleep?'

'Yes, I think s—'

'Mummy, I heard something rattling outside the window.'

'It's probably just the branch of a tree.'

'It's a monster.'

'Of course it isn't a monster.'

'It is. It's a giant anteater.'

'No, it isn't, darling. It'll just be a branch. Do you want Daddy to check?'

'It's just a branch.'

'But it's making a really scary noise, like monster fingers trying to come in.'

'No, it isn't.'
'Can you get rid of the branch, Daddy?'
'No. It's the middle of the night.'
'Pleeeeeease.'

'Did you bring the glass of water?'
'Oh for ffff. No. I'll get it. And then shall we . . .'
'Yes.'

'Alone at last.'
'Yes.'
'Shall we light some candles?'
'No.'
'Okay.'

'Can you just rub my shoulders?'

AFTERWORD

WHAT, SORRY? You're looking for conclusions? A summing up? Of the English? Don't make me. Please don't make me. It's impossible. Have you tried putting English people in a box? Not literally. Health and safety and that. Even metaphorically, the English are not easily pigeon-holeable. No nationality is, except maybe the Swiss. And the Italians. And the Argentinians. But the English are especially tricky. You show me a fifty-year-old Englishman with a bowler hat, a briefcase and an umbrella, and I'll show you another fifty-year-old Englishman with a mohican, a manbag and an ill-advised ring at the end of his nose. He's called Max. He really is. He has no idea when he'll get rid of the mohican. He knows he will be ridiculed when he does even more than when he grew it in the first place. He may have to go to the grave with it. He'll need an extra long coffin.

I do have one little thing to say though. In the course of the last eighteen months of relentless English observing, I have become more convinced that we're not as bad as we think we are. Not in a UKIP-ish this-sceptred-isle-ish, Brussels-is-evil, rule-Britannia type way. But this idea that, compared to the Yanks for example, we have a can-don't attitude, that we're a nation of moaners, whingers, complainers? Didn't get that at all. Almost every single person I doorstepped, cold-called or chased down the high street with a clipboard in the making of this book was warm and friendly and funny. Not at first . . . the English take a while to get going. But even at five in the morning, even stuck behind a 100-truck traffic jam, even in wellies and best Y-fronts in a Norfolk car park at nine at night, the English are quite capable of looking on the bright side.

If you believed the vox pops that crop up on the regional news or in the tabloid press and maybe, very occasionally, the broadsheets too, if you took the lessons of reality television or daytime chat shows as gospel, the English are an angry, curtain-twitching, bigoted and, worst of all, unthinking mob. But in the 8,000 miles of research for this book, I saw not one single pitchfork. And I went everywhere, even Essex. The English make tea, not war. And although we no longer have the imperial arrogance to think we are the best in the world, I'm glad I didn't decide to live my life five minutes from that tropical beach. I would have had a tan but I would also have had children who inflected the end of their sentences and thought Christmas was something you celebrated in the summer.

And now that we're warming to the theme, some other feel-good findings. The much maligned sofa-based existence of the modern English family? Unfair. We're just resting. We're just taking a brief break before we step back into the kitchen, the heart of the home, to microwave delicious, mass-produced curries or, if we happen to be called Jennipher with a ph, wild Alaskan salmon with honey-drizzled carroty carrots and something fluffy for pudding. Forty brief years ago, pasta was considered exotic. Now look at us, filling our trolleys with lemongrass and ginger, smoked garlic, crème fraîche, bish-bash-boshing our way around the planet. And look at us in our gardens and our allotments, gardening and allotmenting. Or, at the very least, barbecuing. Or, at the even leaster than that, sitting in our shed starting a new hobby which will soon be an old hobby which will soon form one-third of a car boot on the way to the Neveden Giant Boot. Or if it's none of those things, then look at us watching all the gardening programmes. It's enough. Ditto home improvements (not counting IKEA tea lights). Ditto the gym. If we're good at one thing, the English, it's delayed gratification. Not of the shopping variety. Nothing will stop that particular, filthy orgy, but sorting out the house/the garden/the man-boobs . . . we'll happily put off those pleasures, sometimes indefinitely.

And look at us at five in the morning, waiting for the train in the drizzle. Look at us with our 8.3 out of 10 moods and our sardonic smiles and our coffees and, on Tuesdays, our sausage bagels. And look at us having our grotty affairs in motels off the M1. Or not having affairs, just buying picnic chairs with our petrol. Or an inflatable boat. Or a six-pack of Fruitellas. Or Michael Ball's greatest hit. We're good at moving around. We can pack three bootfuls of stuff we don't need for our holiday into one boot as long as the kids don't mind having the inflatable boat across their laps and Wife doesn't mind the oars on hers. Yes, road rage. Yes, tail-gating. Yes, you people with your Audis and your Bi-Xenon headlights. But try driving from Rome to anywhere near Rome in the rush *ora*. It will make the M25 feel like *Driving Miss Daisy*.

And yes, the English drink. No escaping that fact. On a weekend, you will find English people, young English people, drinking and falling over and fighting, sometimes on an empty stomach, very occasionally with dangerously full bladders. And yes, the English watch football and foot-ballers are no role models but it's not as simple as that. There is wanton tribalism and the referee is a **** but also you could fall in love with the ritualised trudge to and from the terrace on a Saturday afternoon. Or you could sip your way through a four-pack of supermarket bitter as the baffling ripples of village cricket wash over you. Europe will never understand that and nor will the rest of Britain – but we will never grasp pétanque or that thing those Scottish women do with an ice rink and some brooms.

And so to bed where I have most enjoyed shining an observational light. No, not in the forests of Norfolk. No, not in a disturbingly voyeuristic, please-stop-shining-that-light-through-our-bedroom-window way either. But it is a relief that we are not a nation of 1973 Ronnies, devoid of romance, passion and naughtiness.* Some of you are, quite frankly, outrageous. Most of you approach the joy of a relationship with a sideways smile and the expectation of decline. This couldn't be healthier. In an age of celebrity Botox and an industrial-scale glossy airbrushing scandal, the English still, somehow, know how to grow old and grow together gracefully. Things droop. Other things droop too. And we seem to accept this with a giggle and a dig in the ribs. There are exceptions. Yes, you with the comb-over. Yes, you with the sex dungeon. But, you know, it could be a lot worse, mentioning no names, Silvio Berlusconi.

I'm writing this on a train which is late because of the late running of an earlier service. If I wasn't writing this, it would be the sort of time I might close my eyes and imagine the tropical beach I could have been lying on if I hadn't decided I missed the summer drizzle and the greys and browns, and the long dark nights of winter. I might imagine the fine, bronzed, muscular torso I would have undoubtedly developed if I'd spent the last twenty years living a healthy, outdoorsy lifestyle with my quite hot exotic girlfriend and shrimp for dinner with pineapple for afters. But then I might also have imagined the sand that would have got into my socks which I would still insist on wearing

* To be clear, Ronnie Corbett in *No Sex Please, We're British*, not Ronnie Corbett in real life. I have no idea what he gets up to between the sheets and I have no wish to know either.

on the beach. And it would be very irritating, but not as irritating as the news that it would be very hot and sunny tomorrow and very hot and sunny the day after and very hot and sunny the day after that. And then my trip to the tropical beach would be interrupted by the man next to me phoning his boss to tell him he would be late due to the late-running of an earlier service and the woman opposite me opening a loud packet of cheese and onion crisps even though it's eight in the morning. And life in England would continue as very, very normal.

ACKNOWLEDGEMENTS

My FRIEND AMY, the girl who sat opposite me at work (and never talked too loudly about baseball because she was English, not American), died last July. We had confided in each other about our newspaper stories and, on weekends in late spring, we had worked together on this book. She took my plans for each chapter and pushed them further, and made me talk to naked people and microwave fanatics. She sent me on my new, improved journey and then she went on her own unexpected one, leaving us all behind. I wish she was here today to share a toast over a finished book. I would have liked to thank her in person.

And now to the editors. I wouldn't have got around to starting the book if it wasn't for Annabel Wright, my first editor at HarperCollins, who thought the all-encompassing subject of the English would be great, made me sign stuff and then skipped off to start her own company. I wouldn't have got around to finishing it if it wasn't for my current editor Martin Redfern, a slave-driver in an almost entirely good way. Damn him and his being right about everything, when I think about it. Thank you also to Katherine Josselyn, Kate Tolley, Tara Al Azzawi and Jess Fawcett, gentler whip-crackers at HarperCollins.

My agent, Euan Thorneycroft at A.M.Heath, is the voice of calm at times of panic. He would have been good on the *Titanic*. Let's hope this isn't the *Titanic*. Thanks to him and Pippa McCarthy.

The good people of the *Sunday Times*, not least Sarah Baxter, Alan Hunter, Martin Ivens and John Witherow, have been thoroughly supportive of this most extensive of writing projects. More importantly, so has Mehmet on Platform One with his excellent coffee. But not my 'mate' Martin who has contributed even less in this than in previous tomes. He would go in the unacknowledged section I'm not allowed.

Thank you to all the star interviewees of this book, the mad, funny Englishers who happily opened their doors and their lives to scrutiny when they could have treated me like we treat double-glazing salespeople and just got on with their day. There were 493 of them. All brilliant. Thank you.

And thank you to my family. To Harriet, who has to read everything three times and not be too critical and not be too complimentary, and has been the foil for too many jokes. Ditto A and A. Ditto F, F and E, who are too young to be of any use as proofreaders but kept smiling throughout the last eighteen months of having a largely absentee dad. Though 'kept smiling' is an exaggeration. 'Occasionally smiled' is closer to the truth. We wouldn't want to exaggerate, would we?

In memory of Amy Turner
1982–2012